A DORSET PARISH
REMEMBERS
1914 - 1919

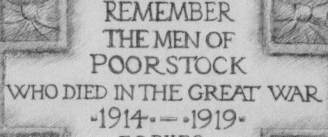

REMEMBER
THE MEN OF
POORSTOCK
WHO DIED IN THE GREAT WAR
·1914· – ·1919·

F.G. BILES
10TH BN HANTS REGT

G. GALPIN
2ND BN DORSET REGT

H. F. HANSFORD
DORSET YEOMANRY

H. MARSH
H.M.S. CARLISLE

R. REED
7TH BN DORSET REGT

W.C.P. STONE
1ST BN DORSET REGT

S.J. STYLES
ROYAL FIELD ARTY

F. SYMES
ROYAL GARRISON ARTY

A. TILTMAN
H.M.S. BLACK PRINCE

F.H.R. TRAVERS
H.M.S. BVLWARK

C. WATTS
15TH BN HANTS REGT

THEIR NAME
LIVETH FOR EVERMORE

A DORSET PARISH REMEMBERS 1914 - 1919

The Parish of Powerstock

Edited by Richard Connaughton

Our Roll of Honour

Most Parishes maintained what is called Our Roll of Honour. The Parish Roll is originally drawn up in three columns, not the two shown here. It begins:

PRAY FOR THOSE WHO HAVE GONE FROM THIS PARISH TO SERVE OUR KING
AND COUNTRY BY LAND AND SEA AND AIR.

The Roll carries the names of men of the Parish who returned from the First World War.

Those Lost appear within the three columns but have also been extracted and recorded separately at the bottom of the original document under the heading:

"THESE HAVE DIED FOR THEIR COUNTRY'S SAKE"

approximately ten per cent of the total. The Ships and Units in which the men served are described here, precisely as shown on the Roll of Honour.

Adams, Albert	3rd Dorsets	Neale, George	HMS Hermione
Ashford, P.H.	RFA Dorset Batt.	Nicholson, H.B.	King's R Rifles
Ashford, William G.	HMS Adamant	Nicol, Robert	HMS Antrim
Baggs, Arthur	Som. Light Infantry	Northover, Charles F.J.	Dorset Yeomanry
Bartlett, Alonzo	RFA Dorset Batt.	Northover, Harold	RAF
Biles, Oscar	8th Warwicks	Northover, Tom J.	Motor Transport
Bush, William W.	5th Lancers	Pickford, William	RMLI
Chubb, Lewis	Wilts	Riglar, Sam	Som. Light Infantry
Cox, Sidney G.	ASC	Rowe, Fredk. W.	ASC
Crabb, Albert V.	Army Service Corps	Russell, H. Lewis	Army Service Corps
Crabb, Charles	5th Dorsets	Sanctuary, A.G.E.	RFA Dorset Batt.
Crabb, George	Army Service Corps	Sanctuary, Charles T.	RFA Dorset Batt.
Crabb, Reg W.	HMS Iron Duke	Sanctuary, H.N.	HMS New Zealand
Crabb, Walter	Kitchener's Army	Score, William	Kitchener's Army 3rd Wilts
Crabb, William W.	5th Dorset RFA	Slade, John	Dorsets
Dawbn.ey, John	3rd Dorsets	Slade, Tom	Dorsets
Forde, Larry	RFA Dorset Batt.	Stevens, Guy	Dorset Yeomanry
Fry, Fred H.	HMS Albion	Stone, Archie	Garrison Artillery
Gale, Edward	3rd Dorsets	Stone, Ernest	1st Dorsets
Gale, Ernest	ASC	Stone, F. John	HMS Albacore
Gale, Frank	Dorset Yeomanry	Stone, Herbert E.	3rd Dorsets
Gale, Harry	4th Dorsets	Stone, William G.	1st Devons
Gale, Leonard	RFA Dorset Batt.	Sykes, Charles	AB Royal Navy
Gale, Oscar	Som. Light Infantry	Sykes, Percy	Terrl. Reserve
Gale, William Charles	RAMC	Symes, Jubilee	R Garrison Artillery
Galpin, Arthur H.	RGA	Symes, Robert	1st Dorsets
Galpin, Charles	Training Reserve	Symes, Walter	Devons
Galpin, Joseph	RFA Dorset Batt.	Travers A. Jesse	3rd Dorsets
Galpin, Richard	Royal Engineers	Travers, James	RFA
Glossop, John	HMAS Sydney	Travers, Richard	R Garrison Artillery
Gough, James	Dorset Territorials	Travers, Willoughby	RN Barracks
Hallett, Frank	RFA Dorset Batt.	Tucker, Henry J.	RMLI
Hallett, Gilbert	RGA	Walburton, Gervais	RMLI
Hilling, M.W.E.	3rd East Surreys	Watts, Edward	RGA
House, Charles	Dorset Yeomanry	Watts, George	Som. Light Infantry
House, Fred	Dorset Yeomanry	Watts, Henry	Durham Light Inf.
Knight, John	HMS Venerable	Watts, William	-
Legg, Charles	Som. Light Infantry	Welch, Percy	3rd Dorsets
Legg, William	RFA	Wheeler, W.F.	Army Ordnance
Lucas, Bat.	RE	White, W.S.	1st Hereford Reserve
Lush, C. Reuben	5th Dorsets	Whitelock, Victor	Dorset Yeomanry
Marsh, Harry	RE	Wiles, Oscar	HMS Kg. George V
Marsh, Sam	HMS Impregnable	Wiles, Stanley	Boom Defence
Marsh, Sidney	R Flying Corps	Wills, Frank	4th Dorsets
Marsh, Thomas	Grenadier Guards	Wood, John	3rd Dorsets
Miller, Oscar	RM Artillery	Wyatt, Richard	Training Reserve

POPPIES

Why, when I see spots of red
in fields of wheat so often seen,
Mexican-waving to me
unthinkingly in the breeze,
do I think, not of bread, but of the dead,
gathered while still green?

"For King and Country" did they die.
Potent totems, stone dead,
stand like sentries, sadly sighing,
stirring questions throughout the land…
where, how, when…why?
On mossy steps we view the scene,
forgotten names now lichen green.

When I see spots of red
in fields of wheat near its prime,
Mexican-waving to me
unthinkingly in the breeze,
I think, not of bread, but of the dead
who died to give me time.

Roger Britton

Published by Milton Mill Publishing, Milton Mill
West Milton, Bridport, Dorset DT6 3SN

First Published in 2014

Printed and bound by Henry Ling Ltd
The Dorset Press, Dorchester DT1 1HD

ISBN 978-0-9540570-3-9

A CIP catalogue record for this book is available from the British Library

TABLE OF CONTENTS

INTRODUCTION

The community which received the news of European war in the summer of 1914 was not a single unified settlement; it consisted of four principal hamlets, Powerstock (formerly known as Poorstock) (Plates 1 & 2), Nettlecombe (Plate 3), North Poorton, and West Milton, and even the largest, Powerstock, lying against the west face of a steep hill, had nothing much in the way of a centre. But the four main institutions which drew people together – the church, the school, the reading room and the pub – were all close together at the four corners of a loose square. Other churches stood at North Poorton and West Milton, and Nettlecombe and West Milton had chapels. West Milton and Nettlecombe also had pubs, the latter still remains. In every direction, small farms stretched over almost 5,000 hilly acres. Bridport, four miles away, is the nearest town, and it is on its newspaper, the *Bridport News*, that the account of the village's wartime experience has largely depended. A record of events before, during and after the First World War appears in the two following Chapters. The reason and justification for undertaking this project are of more recent provenance.

Parishioners had become discomfited on Remembrance Sunday when they assembled to *remember* those who had answered the call to the Colours but had not returned. It was the dawning realisation that they were pretending to remember men completely unknown to them, men who had passed outside the parish's collective memory many years before. The decision was taken to take advantage of the centenary of the outbreak of the First World War as an opportunity to right a wrong.

It was not a simple task to catch up on events a century ago. The task was particularly complicated due to a Luftwaffe attack 7th-8th September 1940 during the Second World War which destroyed two thirds of the personal documents of the men who fought in the First World War. There is also the unavoidable fact that the people we are researching were essentially agricultural workers who, short of winning a Distinguished Conduct Medal or Victoria Cross, were not going to attract the attention of whoever wrote the Regimental War Diary. He who wrote the Regimental History found himself extended recording the names of ten officers killed at the same time and place, unable to find space for the names of the 155 Other Ranks killed or missing in the same engagement.

We were aware of the problems in marshalling the facts, which led us to adopt a number of indirect approaches to tease out factual answers so as not to be entirely dependent upon context. The surnames of those lost in the war are still recognisable among the local community. We came to an arrangement with the *Bridport News* whereby each week for three months, one of our researchers had the freedom of use of the centre pages of the newspaper. Here they told the public what was known of their adopted person's story, illustrated with photographs, paraphernalia and a request for support. The first revelation of the plan was released to the public on 5th December 2013. 'Salute to the Fallen – Book Project on 11 who died in Great War' proved productive. For example:

A husband and wife stopped at Bridport on their way home to Liss in Hampshire. The man picked up the *Bridport News* and shortly said to his wife, "they are looking for you". Diana Wells asked her husband what he was talking about. He showed her the *Bridport News*, the names of the 11 who had been lost and our quest for information. Albert Tiltman who died at Jutland on 31st May 1916 was Diana's grandfather. A substantial amount of useful information came our way.

There was also the case of Chief Petty Officer Harry Marsh, killed in Vladivostok in October 1919. Suzanne Podger telephoned his researcher. She told how she had seen the feature in the newspaper and had wept. The story of the mariner and the possible reason for his death had been passed down through her family. That account is in the book.

Many means were employed for the gathering of information. The genealogy websites proved particularly useful. Varying degrees of difficulty were experienced during the course of preparing an individual's profile. None was more difficult than Private Richard

Reed who enlisted in the Dorset Regiment and transferred to the Wiltshire Regiment. We posted notices on websites for anyone who had a photograph of this Richard Reed in their possession to come forward.

Richard Reed was the twin brother of Brenda Sharp's grandmother. Brenda lives in Gosport. She had made a number of visits to Richard Reed's grave in France. For over a quarter of a century her attempts to find the English war memorial bearing her great-uncle's name proved fruitless. She had been close to Powerstock, having searched villages to the west and north. "I never knew Powerstock existed", she explained. It became her life's quest to find this memorial. She spent many hours on her computer trawling the websites until recently came the Eureka moment! "I still remember with disbelief staring at my computer and the question on the screen, 'has anyone a photograph of Richard Reed?' with contact details". It was her Richard Reed. Brenda and her husband Leo came to Powerstock. She stood there quietly, almost in disbelief as she looked up at the elusive name, 'Richard Reed, 7th Bn Dorset Regt'. She moved forward, placing a posy of blood red camellias from her garden at the foot of the memorial. Job done, and once again an otherwise unexpected flow of information from the family.

When a book has 17 authors it is unwise to get among the weeds and quibble about style and length of paragraphs. Guidance was provided on matters of standardisation. For example, we preferred The First World War to World War One and its diminutive, WW1. There was a ruling on the use of the umlaut, which some might feel is coming very close to the weeds. What matters in the final analysis is the words, their use and meaning.

That the Great War had been the first world war or a component of one larger world war, can be verified by reference to the locations where our Parish's men died: two on the Western Front, two in Gallipoli, two in the United Kingdom and one each in Egypt, at Jutland, in Mesopotamia, Poona and Vladivostok. Almost half – five of the eleven – died through illness or by accident. Their final journeys had begun from what was an insignificant dot on the County Map of Dorset.

The team, for that is what we were, wish to express our grateful thanks and admiration for the contributions of our two guest writers from outside the Parish. To James Crowden for weaving the sublime poetical story of the lost men. James drew the material for each individual's separate verse from the product of research, which he then set in the genre associated with First World War poetry. To Professor David Reynolds whose knowledge and use of words provides a polished and timely reminder why it was thought necessary to write this book – lest we forget. The editor thanks the team, without whose enthusiasm, dedication and curiosity, there would be no book. Special thanks are due to Trevor Ware, enabler and administrator.

Among the many others who came forward, and without whose help this book would not have been possible, we recognise and thank the friends and relatives of those who died and who assisted the Researchers by providing information unavailable elsewhere. We thank the many members of the public met along the way. It is our pleasure also to thank and record the substantial contributions of: Georgina Connaughton, Mary Connaughton, Chris Day, Rene Gerryts, the Keep Military Museum of Devon and Dorset, Channy Kennard, David Risk Kennard, Steve Luck, Margaret Morgan-Grenville and Tracey Brady of The Marquis of Lorne.

CHAPTER 1

The Land They Left Behind

EVEN IN Powerstock, far from the centre of things, the Edwardian Era must have seemed like a golden age after the horrors of the First World War. It had begun when Edward VII succeeded to the throne on the death of his mother, Queen Victoria, in January 1901, and ended with his death in 1910 when King George V succeeded him.

That was the year in which Scott sailed to Antarctica on board the *Terra Nova*, when Old Trafford, Manchester United's famous football ground, opened for the first time in February with a 4-3 defeat by Liverpool, E.M. Forster wrote *Howard's End*, and H.G. Wells wrote *The History of Mr Polly*. It was also the year in which Dr Crippen, having shocked the nation by poisoning his wife and burying her in the cellar, was sentenced to death and hanged in November.

The following year began with a bang in London's East End where the Metropolitan Police and the Scots Guards took on a gang of Latvian criminals in a shootout that became known as the Siege of Sydney Street. In May the ill-fated liner, *Titanic*, was launched in Belfast, and the summer that followed was the hottest on record. It peaked in August when the thermometer reached 98 degrees in Northamptonshire; a record that would remain unbroken until 1990.

In January 1912 came news that Scott's Antarctic expedition had reached the South Pole only to find that Amundsen, the Norwegian explorer, had beaten them to it. In April the entire nation was shocked to hear that the *Titanic* had sunk on her maiden voyage to the USA with tragic loss of life, and the previous year's scorching summer was followed by the wettest August on record.

In 1913 it was the Suffragette movement that generated the headlines when Emmeline Pankhurst was sentenced to three years' penal servitude and Emily Davison ran out in front of the King's horse, Anmer, and was trampled to death.

Then came 1914 and on August 4th the country found itself sleepwalking into war with the Kaiser's Germany. On the very next day, the *SS König Luise*, an Imperial German Navy minelayer, was intercepted in the act of laying a minefield 40 miles off Lowestoft, and sunk by the Royal Naval light cruiser *HMS Amphion*, becoming the first German naval loss of the war. Seventeen days later, a British cavalryman, Drummer Edward Thomas of the 4th Royal Irish Dragoon Guards, became the first man to fire a shot in anger on the European mainland since the Battle of Waterloo.

From end to end Britain was gripped by fears of invasion. At West Bay a beacon was set up on the East Cliff to warn of any possible incursions, and recruiting officers scoured the villages for able-bodied men. As for Bridport, which had a population of about 6,000 at the outbreak of the war, 700 men would embark on active service.

Many West Dorset men had joined the Royal Navy, and the grim realities of war were soon brought home when *HMS Bulwark* was blown up at Sheerness on 26th November 1914, killing Fred Travers, Powerstock's second fatality of the war.

*****

"Isn't this worth fighting for?" asks an enlistment poster of the time. In the foreground stands a British infantryman in full battledress, posing against a background of thatched cottages with roses around the door, a winding country lane and an idyllic vision of green hills, fields and hedgerows. This was the England for which so many of our countrymen fought and died in the trenches. At least, that was the dream; the vision of the land they left behind. But what was it really like? And in particular, what was it like for the men of Powerstock who went off to fight in the First World War and never returned?

In many ways the Dorset we know today has changed out of all recognition in the last 100 years. A century ago it was the poorest, least industrialised county in Britain, still locked in an ancient silence in which life for most of its inhabitants was measured by the eight miles per hour that a horse could cover. At that time some 30 per cent of all farmland was used to feed the horses that were so vital to the nation's economy.

These were the days when Dorset farmers in early spring would stamp out into the soft West Country dawns to follow the plough; and although a million horses would be requisitioned from farms, liveries and hunt stables and sent to the Western Front (of which no more than 60,000 returned), there were still a hundred horses in Powerstock parish in 1917.

It is also worth remembering that the fathers of the men who went off to the Flanders trenches could themselves have fought in the Zulu Wars, and doubtless there were village greybeards – born in the days before Darwin had published *The Origin of Species* – who would have been alive at the time of the Charge of the Light Brigade in 1854.

As for Bridport, which had supplied the nets and rigging for Nelson's navy, its shipyard had been sold in 1879, its heyday long past; but the masts and yards of square-rigged trading schooners still graced West Bay harbour, lying in the shadow of Pier Terrace, which had been built in 1884.

In summer, on farms untouched by the deadly kiss of herbicides, scarlet poppies bloomed in profusion amid the standing corn, as they would on the bloody battlefields where the Great War would soon be enacted.

As yet, barbed wire was still a novelty in the English countryside and so the fields themselves – loud in summer with the sound of bees and grasshoppers – were set about by hedgerows cut and laid by hand, with no tools but the axe, billhook and slasher, creating a stock-proof barrier in the distinctive local style, in which the pleachers (stems) were laid flat along the hedges' alternative sides.

Parish place-names were still common currency – Wynard, Trench and Humpty Castle – as were the names by which every field was known to everyone: Lamp Ground, Butts and Haydish in Powerstock; Gore, Knights Mead and Maiden Crate in West Milton. Today the language of the fields is largely forgotten, although Nick Poole, the West Milton cider maker who grew up on Kings Farm, Eggardon, can still reel off all the names of his father's fields: Long Strip, Church Ground, Middle Mead and Bedvease; and Everard Marsh can do the same at Powerstock Mill Farm, from Knowles Cowleaze and Little Turners Pool to Pitcher's Hill and Lodburn Copse.

In the wet valley bottoms cattle stood up to their udders in buttercups as they grazed contentedly across unimproved pastures dotted with what villagers called *want heaves* and *emmet butts* – mole hills and ant heaps. For this was an age when local people still spoke with a broad Dorset accent, and villagers nursing their pints in The Three Horseshoes would pepper their conversation with dialect words known today only through the poetry of William Barnes.

Above, on the slopes of Eggardon and on the chalk downs beyond, shepherds wandered with their flocks. This was the England described by W.H. Hudson in his rural masterpiece, *A Shepherd's Life*. Published in 1901, it describes rural life on the Wiltshire chalklands but the portrait it paints could just as easily be ascribed to West Dorset, where the upland sheepwalks remained largely unploughed, their skies loud with skylarks and the turf still pristine, rippling with the barrows of Bronze Age kings, its delicate harebells and chalkhill blue butterflies and the long-vanished sound of sheep bells.

Those early years of the 20th century were the heyday of sport shooting, but it came to an end with the outbreak of the war when gamekeepers and their masters went off to fight for king and country. In 1911 more than 23,000 countrymen were employed as gamekeepers in Britain – compared to fewer than 5,000 today. Then came the war. Game management virtually ceased and never completely recovered, allowing persecuted species such as buzzards and sparrowhawks time to recover from centuries of slaughter.

The art of setting gin traps for catching rabbits was widespread and remained legal right up until 1956. Packs of otter hounds, the Cheriton, Culmstock and Courtenay Tracy among them, hunted up and down Dorset's rivers. Fox hunting remained as popular as ever with the gentry and badger baiting continued undercover as a working class pastime even though it had been illegal since the 1830s.

That didn't stop badgers being classed as vermin, along with hedgehogs, stoats, jays, crows and magpies. Even bullfinches and house sparrows were fair game. Yet barn owls still drifted across the meadows at dusk, and every spring the cuckoos called all day long in the valleys. The summer skies were alive with clouds of swifts, swallows and the house martins that built their mud nests under the eaves of every village roof as the cider apples ripened in the orchards.

At the turn of the century there was hardly a farm that did not have an orchard and a cider press. Dorset could boast of 10,000 acres of orchards and Powerstock alone had as many as 135 acres. Here, on the steep little hillsides around Nettlecombe and West Milton, all kinds of local varieties of cider apple trees were grown. Among them were Buttery d'Or, Golden Ball, Sweet Coppin and King's Favourite, and one tree in Powerstock was said to have yielded seven hogsheads in one season – equivalent to nearly 450 gallons. All of it was needed as copious quantities were drunk, especially at haymaking or harvest time when a farm worker might easily put away two gallons a day and cider was included as part of his wages. Now the old orchards lie neglected and overgrown, with only a few greybeard trees left standing, although the art of cider making has enjoyed something of a renaissance over the past decade.

In 1871 there were more than a hundred dwellings in Powerstock, but some were little more than dirt-floored hovels and many disappeared over the next four decades. When the war began there were perhaps 650 people living in the parish, of whom more than 40 were farmers and farm workers who ploughed the fields, hauled hay, threshed corn, mowed grass, trimmed hedges, built drystone walls, beat game for the Manor, harvested bracken for bedding and cut reed for thatching. Their diet was bread and potatoes and blue vinney cheese, supplemented by bacon and pork dripping washed down with tea and beer or hot-pokered cider in winter.

Other residents were employed as wheelwrights, grooms and shepherds or eked out a living as hagglers or rabbit-catchers, and Powerstock still had a cobbler and a blacksmith at the time of the Great War, as well as a slaughterhouse and a baker who had permission to cut firewood for his oven on Powerstock Common, while women supplemented the family income by making nets in Bridport.

In 1906 the Three Horseshoes Inn was rebuilt after fire destroyed the thatched roof, but the village tree, a far-spreading sycamore that stood outside on the other side of the road, continued to cast its generous shade until well into the 20th century.

Fire was a constant hazard in those days, as most cottages had a thatched roof, laid in the plain and functional Dorset style, using longstraw or combed wheat reed to create a flush ridge with little or no fancy ornamentation.

Sewage ran untreated into the Mangerton Brook and villagers relied on wells for water until it was brought from Eggardon in cast iron pipes laid by Captain Nicholson after he came to live at Mappercombe in 1905 – pipes which, incidentally, are still in use today.

Superstitions flourished. Belief in ghosts was widespread and Eggardon at night was alive with spectral figures: Diana the Huntress and her phantom hounds, Roman soldiers, funeral cortèges and even the Devil himself.

Electricity did not arrive until 1935. Before then it was candles and oil lamps, and it would be many more years before the giant pylons of the national grid would despoil the view. Health care was basic – the National Health Service lay decades away in the future – and dentistry was still in its infancy, as was dental hygiene. The toothbrushes issued to all serving soldiers in the First World War were a novelty for most working class men.

*****

It was the coming of the railway that ended Powerstock's feeling of true rural isolation, heralding the end of an epoch in which the horse had been king ever since Vespasian's legions had swept through Dorset 1,700 years ago.

The branch line from Maiden Newton to Bridport and West Bay had opened in 1857, its steam locomotives connecting West Dorset to the outside world in the form of the Great Western Railway who eventually acquired it in 1901. A railway station was built at Smokeham – later renamed Powerstock – and another one built later at Toller Porcorum although, strangely, Loders was completely ignored. During the war, numbers of oak trees were felled in Powerstock Forest and taken direct by wagons up the line that ran conveniently alongside the woods.

By the early 1900s brass-lamped motor cars with solid rubber tyres had begun to venture into Bridport's outlying villages but they were still a novelty, and horse-drawn carts, carriages and delivery vans were still the order of the day. Around Powerstock the roads were maintained by the Gale family, that lived at Knapp Farm and who eventually tarred and chipped the road to Bridport in 1922, using flints dug from the chalky hillsides of Eggardon and stone quarried at Whetley.

Miss Isobel Gale, who died in 1984 at the age of 96, remembered playing with a small boy who used to visit the Vicarage in the years leading up to the First World War. She did not know it then, but that boy would grow up to play a crucial part in the Second World War as Field-Marshal the Viscount Montgomery of Alamein.

Powerstock children – at least a hundred of them in the 1900s – attended the Victorian village school, and in church they sang lustily to the swelling chords of the organ played by Mrs May Daubney, who had arrived in 1910 as a schoolteacher and who continued to play every Sunday for the next 50 years.

From time to time news of important national events would reach Powerstock, such as the Coronation of King George V in 1911, an occasion that was celebrated with a church service followed by a dinner in the Glebe Barn costing two shillings a head, after which everyone hurried off to watch a bonfire being lit on Eggardon Hill.

But only rarely did local drama intrude upon the rural tranquillity of village life. One of the few exceptions was an argument that took place in the summer of 1910 when a scything gang were mowing grass at Whetley and a man was stabbed with a scythe blade. Someone was sent to fetch the doctor from Beaminster but by the time he arrived the man had bled to death – a crime for which the assailant received five years in Dorchester Prison.

Otherwise the years slid by, each season being marked as it always had been. The Mummers came round at Christmas time, enacting their traditional tale of St George and the Dragon. In summertime children were awarded prize money for collecting queen wasps, and anyone lucky enough to take the train down to West Bay could enjoy a sixpenny tea and a minstrel show. But home entertainment was still the norm and village activities thrived in Powerstock: Bible classes, dancing classes, the Mother's Union and the Ancient Order of Foresters.

Such was life in what would soon become known as Hardy's Dorset. Thomas Hardy was aged 70 when the war broke out, his reputation already firmly established as one of the country's most famous novelists. In February 1914 he had married Florence Dugdale, his second wife, and was living at Max Gate in Dorchester and writing his finest poetry.

The war years touched Powerstock in many ways. Towards its

end, villagers making their way into Bridport would have noticed the landmark trees newly planted on Colmer's Hill by Major W.P. Colfox, MC. Another soldier, Harold Norwood, who lived opposite The Three Horseshoes, was blown up in the attack on Hill 60 but survived to live on peacefully into the 1960s. But of course its greatest impact was felt among the families of the eleven men who never returned and whose names are read out with solemn ceremony every year on Armistice Day.

Brian Jackman

Brian Jackman is an author and travel writer who has lived in the parish of Powerstock since the 1960s. His latest book, *Savannah Diaries*, was published by Bradt in February 2014.

Sources:
Powerstock – A Short Social History by H.S. Poole
Poorstock in Wessex by Rosemary Best

CHAPTER 2

Powerstock in War:
A Home Front, 1914 - 19

WAR NEARBY in Europe induced alarm in West Dorset quite unlike the indifference that met the distant imperial wars of the previous decades. The Melplash Show was postponed and considerable anxiety developed over the presence of German agents. Boy scouts were set to guard the water supplies in Dorchester, and James Rennie, a London archaeologist making notes in the autumn sunshine on Eggardon Hill, was arrested as a spy. While the professional army, the Expeditionary Force, was sent to France, a massive recruiting effort got underway, promoted by all in authority from Lord Kitchener to the Mayor of Bridport. Some local men, like William Stone of Nettlecombe, a professional soldier, or Albert Tiltman who'd been in the navy for twenty years were trained and ready,

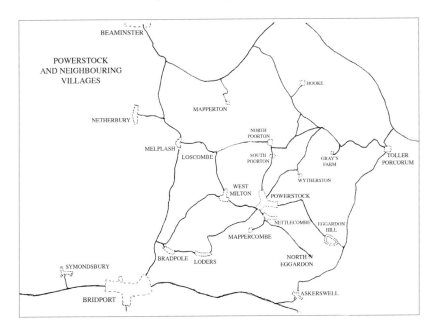

POWERSTOCK
AND NEIGHBOURING
VILLAGES

but several others joined up immediately; by early October there were at least twenty-four volunteers from the village. Most joined the Dorsets – eventually 40 per cent village conscripts were to join that regiment, but several (11 per cent) joined the navy. Other men in their twenties might well have had to travel to find work and, caught up in the enthusiasm of those early months, joined up where the work happened to be. The Watts family of Grays Farm near Wytherston provided soldiers for regiments in Somerset, Hampshire and Durham. And, almost as soon as men began to join up, came the first news of their deaths – for Powerstock the first two came in November.

Much of the land and most of the houses in Powerstock and Nettlecombe were owned either by the Earl of Sandwich or by the Nicholson family who had recently bought the Mappercombe estate. The elderly Lord Sandwich took an interest in the school and visited it occasionally, and had rebuilt several of his village properties, but he lived in distant Huntingdonshire, whereas Captain and Mrs Nicholson at Mappercombe took a generous and detailed interest in the wellbeing of the village. When the Mothers' Union collected £10 for warm clothing for the troops in December 1914, it was to Mrs Nicholson that they presented it. It was to their house that the school children went for tea on New Year's Eve. Annie Rickman, the vicar's wife took a similar leading role, and she convened a meeting in the Reading Room in October of women in the village to hear a series of talks on 'Women and the War'. She also used the Reading Room for a fortnightly Sewing Guild to make comforts for the troops, and later on the Vicar, Rev William Rickman, gave talks there on the progress of the war, starting with one on the Retreat from Mons. The Reading Room, although closed for its usual purpose for the duration of the war, was the scene of many lectures, and as a meeting place it was a precursor to the Hut, given by Captain Nicholson for use as the Village Hall in 1921. There were several courses of lectures on aspects of farming, and it was there that the parish's Women's Institute came into existence in 1917. One activity in which the village made a sustained and considerable effort was in the National Egg Collection, providing fresh eggs for wounded soldiers. Proceeds were delivered to Bridport Town Hall, and must have resulted in considerable problems of transport. In one week in 1915 for example, Powerstock provided 171 dozen eggs, while

Loders produced 65½, and Bridport itself 223, *dozen*.

This part of the country was far away from battlefields; it did not suffer the bombardment that afflicted Scarborough, Whitby and Hartlepool in January 1915, nor the later bombing of London. Nor was the noise of the guns on the Western Front audible as it was in Kent. Nevertheless the war was real in other ways than simply being responsible for ensuring the personal sacrifice of so many men. A prisoner of war camp was set up at Dorchester, initially for the crews of captured German ships, and then a further 500 prisoners arrived in December 1914. At the coast too, bodies of British sailors were washed up at Burton Bradstock and Lyme following the sinking of *HMS Formidable* on New Year's Day. Soldiers home on leave had their own stories to tell. Private Robert Symes, of The Lane, West Milton, was invalided home from service with the 1st Dorsets, who had fought through the whole of the last dispiriting months of 1914, ending in the First Battle of Ypres. He contracted frostbite, and after treatment at a hospital in Manchester he came home, to give a wonderfully upbeat account of his experience.

Powerstock School had about 100 pupils; all came from the parish and were bound far more closely into village life, and so to its experience of war. The children collected money for the Overseas Club to provide 'comforts', later described as 'tobacco and comforts', for 'our brave soldiers': 9s 2d in 1915, 10s 8d (in 2014 worth at least £30) in 1916. They also gave a similar sum towards the Jack Cornwell fund following the famous boy VC's death at the Battle of Jutland. Sometimes their generosity was answered by the arrival of postcards back from the front. Empire Day was a major patriotic event for the children: 'special lessons were taken on Patriotism and the splendid devotion to our people at home and abroad during the present crisis', or, as the 1917 School Log more laconically put it, 'Talks of our Empire. The great struggle. duties. etc'. There were treats as well, mostly provided by the vicar. On Prize Day, at the start of each year, he, or perhaps the Nicholsons, provided each child with a bun and an orange, and in the summer he and his wife arranged to take everyone to West Bay to play on the beach, with transport provided in the wagons of local farmers. Attendance, which was the main concern of the School Log, was very variable: contagious illnesses could decimate numbers, as could impassable roads for children walking to school. One burning hot day in August 1916, fewer than half the school were present. The hay harvest, another cause of absence, was finished but the Dorset Regiment were staging manoeuvres on Eggardon, having arrived at Powerstock Station in the morning, and children flocked to that.

As the war continued inexorably its impact on this remote village tightened. Volunteers provided insufficient manpower for the war, yet the creation of the huge New Army created labour shortages at home and the threat to diminished food supply made its effect felt even on the farms. The introduction of conscription early in 1916 brought with it Tribunals at which appeals against military service could be tested. While the few objectors to war on grounds of conscience are well known, the less controversial routine business of the tribunals casts light on conditions in the village where almost everyone was engaged in agriculture, and so on work that could be seen as of 'national importance', and many were in situations where they provided the only income for a young family or an elderly parent. Mr Tom House of Glebe Farm came before the Tribunal in March 1916. He claimed he needed all four sons working for him, but struck a deal whereby Duncan could stay as a shepherd with Thomas James, while Fred and Charles joined up immediately. Many cases of farm carters claiming exemption from military service underlines the importance of the small-scale nature of rural transport. Hamilton George Legg, of Nettlecombe, Albert Bush at Mappercombe, Thomas Lathey near Castle Lane, Oscar Harold Gale of the Knapp, and William Thomas in North Poorton, all carters, gained temporary exemption. Other trades too could claim need: James Biles (21) of Whetley, 'hurdler, thatcher, crib maker and sheep shearer' gained a temporary exemption, just a month before the death of his brother Fred in distant Gallipoli. In May 1916 Hugh Leaf (31), 'shoeing and general smith' gained a conditional exemption, just as his elderly father William, a veteran of the Crimean War and the Indian Mutiny, suffered a fall in his bedroom from which he died a month later. Some could claim no 'need' at all. Two brothers, Thomas (29) and John (20) Slade, farm labourers of West Milton, had to be arrested by PC Vatcher (from Nettlecombe) for refusing to answer two notices to report to the recruiting officer. They were accused of a lack of patriotism, protesting 'this was a free country and as they had nothing to fight for they took no notice of orders'. They were quickly sent off to the

3rd Dorsets, where, it was later reported, 'they have both seen a good deal of active service'.

It is hard to reach an exact number of men from the parish who underwent military service, for the Roll of Honour has several omissions. In Nettlecombe for example, working from the census of 1911, already out of date at the introduction of compulsory military service in 1916, it appears that there were about 35 men of military age in a population of about 173 of which one can only account for the war service of 14. Several others may well have joined up, but the rest were either unfit for military service, like young Edward Score who severed his thumb and forefingers while cutting roots at Mappercombe, or gained exemption.

As the men went off, the women increasingly took their place, even if some farmers found this difficult to accept. In May 1917 the paper reported that there 'were now a great number of women trained for land work' and 'some dozens' had already begun. It appealed to 'village women' to register their services with the village Registrar, whose name would be found in the Post Office. Mrs Nicholson and Mrs Rickman again took the lead at a meeting 'with a very large attendance' to encourage volunteers. Awareness of the increasingly public role of women in the community, obvious from the earliest months when they had met in the Reading Room to listen to a talk on Women and the War, was now shown in many money raising efforts and lectures from the Ministry of Food on the 'special need for economy in the present time'. The formation of the Women's Institute in the autumn of 1917 did much to focus on the domestic economy; at a meeting to discuss 'What is most needed in Powerstock' in May 1918, they felt the greatest need was for a local co-operative market. Land Girls must have come to help the village war effort, though the only one I know of was arrested for stealing a pair of silver sugar tongs, worth 12s 6d, from Lynch Farm, West Milton.

In July 1916 an Open Air Patriotic Meeting was held 'under the large sycamore tree in the centre of the village', to hear a powerful speech by the vicar and, as was the case in Bridport, they took a resolution 'declaring their inflexible determination to continue the struggle to a victorious end'. But the increasing shortage of food, not to mention the steady sequence of notices of dead and wounded men known to them all, placed increasing pressure on the community. The

Dorset War Agriculture Committee tried to promote potato growing. Seed potatoes were distributed throughout the county, and steam ploughing was advocated to break up the ground in preparation. In June 1917 the Parish Council invested in two knapsack sprayers and materials for the making of Burgundy mixture, an early fungicide, but results were slightly disappointing: the county produced 12,300 tons of potatoes in 1917/18, but consumed 20,200. From before the war the school had encouraged gardening, and in March 1915 the boys were given a lesson in pruning the new currant bushes. By the end of the war they were out gathering blackberries – in one week in September 1918 they found 199lbs. The War Agriculture Committee increasingly advocated the use of schoolboy labour and those under fourteen could expect 10s for a 52-hour week. But compulsory rationing arrived in 1918, and in January the Mayor of Bridport warned that butchers would only be allowed to sell half the amount of meat they had sold three months earlier. Whether rationing was at all enforceable in a country parish is another matter.

What might be considered ordinary life in the village went on, of course. When Miss L.M. Attoe, teacher at the school, married Richard, the youngest son of Malachi Dawbeny of Manor Farm, North Poorton, the children presented her with a 'very beautiful' butter dish. Her going-away dress was described as 'n----- brown'. An old sailor, Robert Guppy was found lying on the pavement in Barrack Street, in a hopeless condition; Gilbert Stone of Nettlecombe went to prison for theft. An inquest was held in The Three Horseshoes into the sudden death of Miss Thurza May (61), who helped her elder sister in the shop. She had died of heart failure. The first cuckoo of 1915 was heard on May 22nd. Into this rural world came the grievous letters from commanding officers: the sad death of Gunner Fred Symes of Chapel Cottage, West Milton; of Lance Corporal Victor Darby, wounded in July 1917 by splinters from an exploding shell, who came home in September to marry Miss Lathey of Powerstock and returned to France where he was killed just before Christmas, or about John Stone of Nettlecombe, on *HMS India*, torpedoed in Norwegian waters. He was fortunate: he managed to swim ashore and was interned there. Under an arrangement between governments, Stone managed to enjoy a month's leave at home in September 1917. When Albert Tiltman was lost on *HMS Black Prince* at the battle of Jutland, the bellringers rang a muffled peal 'in memory of our brave sailors lost in the North Sea Battle'.

Bell ringing was forbidden by the Defence of the Realm Act (though, according to the Parish Magazine in 1916, in an air raid a bell would be rung to tell everyone to extinguish their lights). Almost the only other occasion on which they seem to have been rung was on the death of the Earl of Sandwich in the summer of 1916 when the Dead March from *Saul* was played at the following Sunday service. The death of the Lord of the Manor unleashed significant changes in the parish. He had tried to dispose of his great estate based on Hooke before the war; now, with the impact of Estate Duty, this became essential. The following year North and South Poorton Farms, Luccas and King's Farms, and Manor Farm in Powerstock were all sold. Several may have been bought by speculators, for they were quickly sold again. Faced with new owners, and no doubt increased rents, the tenant farmers sold up. Malachi Dawbeny sold his stock, including his eleven fine carthorses at Manor Farm, North Poorton. Six year old 'Jewel, got by Melplash Society's Horse Team – Friar Tom', 16 hands, sold for 143 guineas (at least £6,311 in 2014). Two months later, John Wyatt sold the stock at Manor Farm Powerstock, including the renowned flock of 280 Hampshire Down ewes. This was just a part of a widespread local trend: the Syndercombe and Court Farm estates in Askerswell (1781 acres), Mangerton Manor, and large estates in Symondsbury, Loders and Bradpole were all sold.

The old world was coming to an end on a larger stage too. The *Bridport News* reported the troubles in Ireland and then gave just a quarter of a column to 'Serious News from Russia. Faced with Anarchy and Civil War'. The great German offensive opened in late March 1918 and weekly figures appeared for tonnage lost to unrestricted U Boat warfare. The King inspected the newly arrived American troops. And, at long last, came the 'End of the World War'. The news was brought to the Parish by a wireless message from Paris to the Royal Naval Airship Station at Powerstock (Drackenorth) at 6.30 am on that day. In Powerstock,

'The good news was received with great rejoicing on Monday morning. The Union Jack was at once hoisted on the Church tower and a general display of bunting throughout the village soon followed. The ringers gave several merry peals on the bells. The Vicar and Mrs Rickman visited the school and the children were given an afternoon's holiday (Plate 35). In the evening a special thanksgiving service was held in the parish church attended by a very large congregation'.

The return of men of the 2nd Dorsets who had been in prison in Aleppo since the siege of Kut in 1917 was balanced by news for Mr and Mrs Hamilton Legg in Nettlecombe that their son, who had only been in France for five weeks, had been wounded on 5th November, and had had his left foot amputated.

Demobilised servicemen gradually returned to find the 'Khaki' election in full swing: the Conservative member for West Dorset was returned unopposed. The country, as much of Europe, enfeebled by years of privation was prey to 'Spanish Influenza' first mentioned in May 1918. In fact Powerstock does not appear to have suffered very much, although the school was closed for two months. The average number of burials in the decade before the War had been about eleven, while for the decade after the average was only just over nine, and there was no spike in the numbers during 1918–20. The real celebration came with the signing of the fateful Peace Treaty at Versailles at the end of June 1919.

On the day Powerstock chose for jubilation it rained, and the sports had to be cancelled. Nevertheless a grand lunch took place in the Glebe Barn, lent by Mr Tom House, after which everyone went over for a service in church. Later in the evening there were fireworks on Eggardon and dancing to the Powerstock band. A victory dinner was held in the Bull Hotel, Bridport for the Royal Naval Toller Airship Station which had been based at Drackenorth – the level field at the top of Mount Pleasant in Wytherston, and some of the staff had been billeted with the Watts Family, whose three eldest boys were away at the war. As part of the festivities they now sang:

> You love the Toller mud, I own,
> You love the Toller rain
> You like the barn at Wytherston
> And every windy lane.
> You love each comfortable Hut
> That's been so useful here,

You're very, very happy BUT
You like a little cheer
That's why you're at the Bull tonight
To make you happy and keep you bright.

In April 1917 the vicar had hoped that 'at the end of the war some form of permanent memorial will be erected in the parish recording the names of those who have given their lives for their country'. Now the same thought preoccupied every town and village. In some, discussion was long and difficult; others quickly arrived at their preferred course of action. Askerswell decided to install a new organ which was ready in October 1919, with the names of the fallen inscribed on it. Melplash and Yetminster opted for new pulpits similarly inscribed. Many, including Symondsbury, Portesham, Charmouth and Netherbury erected a cross. A few, like Axminster hoped to erect a village hall, but couldn't raise enough money. Discussions at Powerstock are not recorded, but the result was the unobtrusive bronze tablet on Hoptonwood stone installed towards the end of 1920, and probably unveiled on Remembrance Day in November. At exactly that time Major Nicholson was making his second initiative for the village – he had installed the reredos in the church in 1916 – with the building of the original Hut, and it is likely that this was also seen as a memorial, although he made no mention of this in his speech inaugurating the Hut in November 1921. Six months earlier Charles Galpin, the village carpenter, had made the 'three carved oak panels' for the school, engraved with the names of all the men of Powerstock parish who had served in the war, which was unveiled by Major Nicholson at a 'Warriors Day' in May 1921. The Vicar's speech of thanks included a reference to 'future generations would have in the Roll of Honour a permanent record of the men who answered their country's call in the hour of need'. Sadly, the carved panels have not survived for their centenary.

The commemoration of the dead was on everyone's mind, and communal action in the ubiquitous unveiling of memorials over these months may have done something to assuage the grief of loss. The care of the survivors may have been a far harder task, accomplished, especially in the first few years, largely in silence, and by silence. The newspapers give ample evidence of the widespread relief after the armistice, with dances everywhere. Dancing lessons were provided at the school in the evenings. But when Alfred Hamilton Gale, labourer of Nettlecombe and late of the Labour Battalion, was caught stealing turnips from a field belonging to Charles Crawford, the farmer of Mappercombe in the winter of 1919, and when Crawford spoke in his defence at the trial saying that 'the man had lately gone wrong in his head', we may perhaps be looking at a case of what we might now call Post Traumatic Stress Disorder. Now a treatment may be available; then there was only silence, and desperation. The lasting injuries, nightmares and suffering of some of those who returned are not recorded.

It has recently been said that 'clergymen were widely seen to have become the mouthpiece of the state in promoting patriotic propaganda designed to coerce young men into the forces'. While this may have been true in some places, it pays scant respect to the situation in this small community. The generosity and wide range of activities of William Rickman (Plate 36), Vicar of Powerstock, show how he did everything he could for the welfare of all the village as well as to help the prosecution of a war which almost the entire community thought was just. He and his wife worked tirelessly for the good of all parishioners, whether in promoting the establishment of a Parish Nursing Service, or organising the Sewing Guild, in frequent visits to the school and giving the children outings to the seaside, in urging women to voluntary work, or organising the spraying of potatoes against blight: he did what he could. He died very suddenly in 1924, and his son was killed in the Spanish Civil War.

Rickman was also no doubt the man best situated to compile the Roll of Honour and the list of the Fallen for the memorial in the church. There seem to be inaccuracies in both. To the Roll of Honour another fourteen names might be added to the published 103, and the criteria for inclusion among Powerstock's dead is not always obvious. Fred Travers, blown up in *HMS Bulwark* in 1914 was born in Loders, and had no clear link with Powerstock, yet he appears on memorials in both villages, while Captain Charles Lloyd Sanctuary MC (Plate 37), who grew up in the village where his father was vicar, died of his wounds in France in November 1916, but is remembered on the Frampton War Memorial, perhaps because his father became vicar there the following year, and so was present when the names for that village's memorial were being considered. John Legg of

Mythe, on the border between North Poorton and Mapperton, who went down with *HMS Invincible* at Jutland (in 90 seconds) has no local memorial at all. Only if all names on all memorials could be identified and, in the age of the computer, brought together, would we be able to assess how complete our memory and commemoration are. Perhaps that should be our work of remembrance. Only some of their names live 'evermore'.

Tim Connor

Tim Connor is a retired school teacher. Since arriving in West Dorset he has researched a variety of topics in the history of West Dorset.

Sources:
National Archives, Kew: 1911 Census
Dorset History Centre, Dorchester
Powerstock Parish Magazine, 1913, 1915 - 1918
Powerstock School, Log Book, 1897 - 1970
Powerstock School, Admission Book, 1850 - 1884
Powerstock Register of Burials, 1895 - 2008.
Bridport News, 1914 - 1921

CHAPTER 3

The Reasons Why

IT IS reasonable to want to know what was responsible for taking our peaceable, content, country people away from familiar ridge-lined fields – strip lynchets – and damp combes to the face of war. The parish Roll of Honour reveals 103 men answered the call, of whom 11 died. A loss of 10 per cent is a common proportion across the country although it is said some 54 villages, dubbed the Thankful Villages, saw all their men return. The parish lost four men in the Second World War. This disparity between the numbers killed in the two World Wars requires explanation although it is the common experience of parishes to have lost twice as many men in the First World War as they did in the Second World War. 10 million of all nationalities died in the First World War, 95 per cent servicemen, five per cent civilians. 50 million died in the Second World War, 52 per cent servicemen, 48 per cent civilians. However, British military fatalities in the First World War were 720,000 compared with 382,700 in the Second World War.

The parish Roll of Honour is subordinate in comparison to the war memorial, not least because it is out of sight, out of mind. Yet in some cases, the finality of death might have been preferable for a number of the living dead. The Roll of Honour does not reveal who returned home deaf, blind, limbless, suffering shell shock or associated traumatic stress, or terminal illness arising perhaps from multiple gassing. It is so much to the credit of those who survived the war yet were permanently disabled who just got on with their lives. There is the story of Charlie Legg, formerly of the Somerset Light Infantry, who rejoined Powerstock village cricket club at war's end. Visitors were full of admiration for the way in which he faced their fastest bowlers without having taken the precaution of padding up. He had a wooden right leg. Charlie lost his leg in an explosion on 13th November 1918 – two days after the Armistice. As part of his rehabilitation he was taught to weave baskets. One sentence by Derek Winter I read in the University Alumni Magazine accurately expressed the sentiment that war memorials represent not just the dead but all who served: 'I suggest that the memorials should be seen in a representative way as acknowledging not only the battlefield dead, but also the whole generation who sacrificed much in many different ways in both world wars'. One particularly has in mind women unable to make a suitable marriage and who faced a life of involuntary spinsterhood as well as those women who, out of despair, reluctantly entered into unsuitable marriages.

The First World War had not been a global war in the same way the Second World War would be. It was the lot of a number of our parishioners to have died in far-flung places about which they may never have heard in geography lessons in the village school. It would have been difficult for them to comprehend that battlefields thousands of miles apart were embraced under the one common title, the same war: The First World War. Among the places where they died were Gallipoli, Mesopotamia, Vladivostok, Poona and Egypt. Two of the 11 died on the Western Front. The causes of this war have been expressed simply – over simply – as due to capitalism, imperialism and nationalism. However, the three 'isms' do not stand the test of events at the time.

If reliance is placed upon the literature, it can be difficult to decide where precisely the guilt for the war lies. There is no consensus. Yet, if you happened to be reading a whodunit and curiosity and impatience to identify the villain proves overwhelming, the obvious solution is to turn to the back of the book. The same result can be achieved by turning to clause 231 in the Versailles Peace Treaty Report of 1919. There you will discover the 'guilt' clause where the allies and the Germans agree, the guilty party was Germany. Such a conclusion cannot be easily discounted as symptomatic of victors' justice. Even without affording Germany's domestic politics due consideration, there is a sufficiency of other factors which follow, to be certain that war guilt has been correctly attributed to Germany. Theirs was, however, a limited admission of guilt, being confined to civilian loss and damage.

Relative to knowing the causes of the First World War today, considerably less is known of the course of the war. Many is the number able to identify some of the causes, but ask those same people about Mons or the Battle of the Marne and their significance to the course of the war and few will have answers. What we are doing here is comparing bad with worse cases. A recent YouGov poll revealed 20 per cent of those questioned were unaware we were fighting the Germans. A majority believed we declared war in 1914 due to Germany invading Poland rather than Belgium. Thankfully, discussing the causes of the First World War is a simpler task than discussing the course of the war.

The reasons for the collapse of the Concert of Europe, an international security device overseen by the five principal powers to emerge after the Napoleonic Wars, provide an early inkling of the causes of the First World War. The greater members of the Club were Britain, France, Prussia, Austria and Russia. They had no Charter, no veto, but a preparedness if necessary to trim what were their own national interests to achieve consensus. With the exception of limited, mostly one-on-one conflicts, they maintained peace in Europe for almost a century. It was this fact of having had almost a century of peace that the First World War and its nature had a more pronounced shock on European society than did the Second World War. That the First World War failed in its purpose to be the war to end all wars confirmed its pointlessness. At the time, many thought war to be possible but among the British, a majority believed a war more likely in Belfast than Flanders.

London was aware of Berlin's domestic difficulties. By 1913-14, the money required to sustain their army and navy could not be found through taxation, therefore the solution to preventing a halt to naval expansion and reducing the strength of the army was – to go to war. On balance, the external factors were identifiable as the dominant factors since they reflected Germany's opinion of where she rightfully believed she stood and the need to make that point to the world.

The members of the Concert of Europe understood where their writ ran and at the outset, member states enjoyed an approximate equivalence of power. Towards the end of the 19th century the pre-existing cosy relationship became unstable due to changes in the equivalence of power among the original powers and the emergence of the United States of America as a world power. The USA, despite her preference for isolationism, could not be ignored. It was President Theodore Roosevelt who came forward to adjudicate the 1905 peace treaty between Russia and Japan, for which he was awarded the Nobel Peace Prize at the cost of having confirmed the USA as Japan's natural enemy in the Pacific. The rise of Germany, their GNP enhanced by assets from Alsace Lorraine, advances in industry and technology, reflected in the development of arms and ammunition, set her apart as a new, forward-looking state with no laurels to rest upon. The common denominator affecting all states and how they interacted was the development of global communications. The result saw expansion beyond the former European area of operations into new, wider areas where states sought to create a presence, develop trade and make new treaties, among the first of which was the 1902 Anglo-Japanese Treaty.

A digression is justifiable to examine the advances made in global communication compared with battlefield communications at the tactical and operational levels of war. There, troops were released from their traps in their tens of thousands into the chaos of attacks from which they could not be recalled, could not be moved to the left or the right, or call down defensive fire. The best communication device available was the field telephone and its highly vulnerable land line. "Once you were over the top", said one who had made the journey, "fear left you, to be replaced by terror". Of those who went over the top, one in three was killed or wounded. The allies, proactive in the attack, required in number terms a ratio of three to one, meaning the rule of thumb had it that the beating of one defender was calculated as requiring three attackers. This suggests that the way to win this war was to favour defence over attack in order to achieve 'maximum slaughter at minimum expense'. That truth would be borne out throughout the duration of this war of attrition for, in every month from August 1914 to the summer of 1918, the Germans killed or took as prisoners of war more British and French soldiers than they lost. Why did Germany not win? There were other factors to take into account – logistics, morale and the reality that there were the armed forces of other states in support of the British Empire forces and French, notably the Americans whose war began in 1917.

Otto von Bismarck of Prussia was fearful of war on two fronts. The priority he gave to the shuffling of the component states of the new Germany post-1871 into a harmonised whole, emphasised the domestic paradigm: he was not greatly in favour of foreign adventures. Historians may challenge that claim, asking for a rationale for the apparent paradox of Bismarck's colonial acquisitions 1884-85. The answer is that Bismarck was not set upon the creation of an overseas empire but was sending Britain the clearest of messages that Germany had become a superpower and required to be acknowledged by Britain as such. Bismarck's preoccupation with organising and consolidating the home base on the Junker model was at variance with the Kaiser's wishes. The Kaiser demanded an expansionist *weltpolitik* based on Berlin. Bismarck's disinterest in doing so saw the Kaiser drop the pilot in favour of a new Chancellor, von Bülow, who said: "we don't want to put anyone else in the shade but we too demand a place in the sun". The places in the sun had almost entirely been taken, meaning if Germany were to find her place in the sun, it would involve the displacement of other states, namely Britain and France. Four years into von Bülow's Chancellorship, the French and Russians formed an alliance – two potential German enemies on two fronts.

Kaiser Wilhelm II was the eldest grandson of Queen Victoria and first cousin of King George V and Czar Nicholas II of Russia. Britain and Russia joined France to create the Triple Entente facing the Triple Alliance or Central Powers of Germany, Austria-Hungary and Italy. Italy withdrew from the alliance before the onset of the First World War on the grounds of Austria's oppression of the Serbs and was replaced numerically by Turkey, the so-called 'sick man of Europe'. Those who would fight at Gallipoli did not find the Turkish army at all sick.

Damaged at birth, his left arm barely functional, is one reason believed to have contributed to the Kaiser's strange, strained interpersonal relationships. His purpose was to dominate Europe and ultimately the world. He ensured a great fleet was built to challenge the Royal Navy's supremacy, not that he had any intention the two navies would fight. Germany therefore had assembled a large modern fleet and a large modern army. Britain had the larger fleet but, as the Kaiser remarked, the Royal Navy did not run on wheels. The British Achilles heel was "this contemptible British army". By the end of 1914, little survived of the 150,000-strong British Expeditionary Force.

Britain had a treaty obligation to guarantee the inviolability of

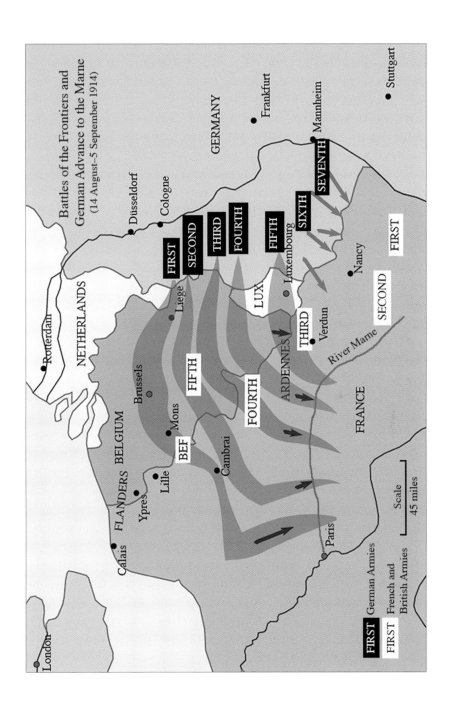

Battles of the Frontiers and
German Advance to the Marne
(14 August–5 September 1914)

Belgian territory, an agreement signed in 1839 by Britain, France and Prussia. The Kaiser did not understand Britain's moral obligation, which she would honour because, quite simply, it was a matter of honour. He, personally, held a fond hope Britain would choose to be neutral, yet there was not a single German military assumption that saw Britain as neutral. As British Foreign Secretary Sir Edward Grey explained to the Commons on 4th August 1914, "the British Empire could either not go to war, suffer badly and be dishonoured or, go to war, suffer badly and not be dishonoured".

By Christmas 1912, Berlin was convinced of the inevitability of war. Of the treaty states, Germany only had need to invade Belgium in her advance into France. Holland remained neutral. Albrecht's Fourth and the Crown Prince's Fifth Army passed through Luxembourg. The invasion of Belgium was essential to find the space required to execute the turning movement intended to encircle Paris in addition to taking control of the railway which would deliver the German Armies and their logistics to their start lines. The plan required the neutralisation of the strategic Belgian fortress at Liège. The Kaiser still held out hope there would be no British reaction – until, that is, their declaration of war on Germany disabused him of that idea.

In attributing the cause of the First World War to Germany, it is an incontrovertible fact that the 1905 Schlieffen Plan, not a contingency plan, was a plan for a deliberate attack, striking westward into France with a view to defeating France in six weeks. Phase 2 was then to deploy the German Army eastward to confront and defeat a notoriously slow to mobilise Russian Army. There was no Plan B. The Schlieffen Plan was simplicity itself, by-passing the strongly defended Franco-German border and entering northern France through Belgium. The German Army was to move far to the west then execute a wheel southwest of Paris, its strong right wing enveloping and capturing Paris, thus bringing the French phase to its timely, planned conclusion. The weakness of the Plan was the optimistic, unrealistic calculation of the time required to complete specific phases. General Schlieffen had made insufficient provision for what the strategist Clausewitz described as friction, the fog of war. General Schlieffen died in 1913. The weakness of his plan was further amplified by Chief of Staff von Moltke's tinkering with detail, thus rendering a simple plan more complex.

The Schlieffen Plan had a use-by date of 1916, brought about by the consideration of domestic politics and the German overestimation of the extent of the rising economic and military strength of Russia. The Russian Army was of relatively poor quality, yet due to the fact their fully mobilised Order of Battle was counted in the millions, there came a point where quantity attracted its own quality. Germany solved that problem in 1917 by setting Lenin down in the Russian centre of gravity, from where he seized power.

The Schlieffen Plan was one of three attacks launched out of Germany upon France over the period 1870-1940. The first of these was in response to a French declaration of war on Prussia in 1870. The Schlieffen Plan was the only one of the three to fail. This was due to Klück's First Army turning eastward prematurely to support von Bülow's Second Army held in check by the French. In so doing, the German right flank became exposed, allowing the French and British to counterattack at the Marne, arguably the world's most decisive battle since Waterloo, initiating the commencement of a stalemate and precipitating digging-in which would last four years. The three weeks of battle here had cost both sides half a million men killed, wounded or captured.

It is probable that if both sides had been aware how long the war would last and how much damage would be inflicted upon both sides, the fateful steps to war would have been avoided. The majority on both sides were convinced that the war would be of short duration and that they would all be home by Christmas 1914. If Schlieffen's Plan had been conducted as intended – his dying words in 1913 were said to have been "keep the right wing strong" – the capitulation of France might have been achieved in six weeks, as was the case a quarter of a century later. Among those who believed the short war scenario to have been hugely optimistic was Britain's Foreign Secretary, Sir Edward Grey who said: "The lamps are going out all over Europe. We shall not see them lit again in our lifetime".

The incident which took Europe over the brink to war was the murder on 28th June 1914 of the heir to the Habsburg throne, Austria's Archduke Franz Ferdinand with his wife in Sarajevo, Serbia (Plate 4) by a Bosnian, a subject of Austro-Hungary, the anarchist Gavril Princip. It had not been a sensible day for the Austrian couple to drive through Sarajevo in an open car. In Kosovo on 28th June 1389, a Turkish victory brought Serbian independence to an end. There were indicators Franz Ferdinand might be subjected to an assassination attempt. The first attack occurred that morning when a bomb injured one of the archduke's entourage. It was whilst on his way to make an unscheduled visit to the hospital that the chauffeur lost his way in the city's narrow streets. These were dangerous streets. Serbs had undergone extensive weapons training in preparation for this moment. The royal car passed close by Princip but not close enough for him to bring his revolver up into a firing position. It was bad luck which brought the returning royal car alongside where Princip was sitting. He did not fail again.

The question now requiring an answer was what to do with Serbia or to Serbia. Germany encouraged Austria to do something. Austria was lethargic and Hungary uninterested. The complication here lay in Russia's position as defender of the rights of Slavic people. Lorrainer French President Raymond Poincaré was in St Petersburg at the time of the assassination. Vienna decided to take no action until Poincaré was safely en route in the Gulf of Finland. An ultimatum was penned and delivered on 23rd July. The 10 demands were so provocatively demanding as to be transparently obviously to be begging rejection. Austria gave Serbia 48 hours to reply. With one minor objection, Serbia agreed to all Austria's demands. Austria rejected Serbia's reply and decided upon the path to war if only, in their mind, to preserve the Habsburg Empire and prevent the unification of the South Slav race. An envoy was sent from Vienna to Berlin to explain Austria's position and seek confirmation of Germany's support. The answer would determine whether there would be a major or minor war. If the crisis was dealt with swiftly and Germany acted as the honest broker between Austria-Hungary (Hungary was now on-side) and Russia, the conflict would be localised. At this point it is possible to identify Germany as responsible for the outbreak of war. Berlin gave Vienna a cast iron promise of support. Von Moltke was particularly active, telling Austria to "get on with it". The German navy and army were at their peak in terms of equipment and manpower, a situation which could change. Aware that their decision would probably trigger Russian mobilisation, Germany decided to proceed. Russia prepared to mobilise her forces in European Russia. "Good", said a German General, "the war can now begin by itself". The rest of

Europe awoke, now aware that this was not just another Balkan crisis. Britain's Foreign Secretary Grey attempted to convene a great power conference to halt the ponderous momentum towards war. Germany refused to cooperate, insisting the matter was best addressed through direct negotiations between Austria and Russia.

Russia did not want to go to war. It was debatable whether the Reichstag would provide the war credits to allow Germany to go to war. The only possible justification was to persuade the politicians the Reich was in danger. On 28th July, Austria declared war on Serbia. Russia began a partial mobilisation. Von Moltke put pressure on Austria to declare a general mobilisation. On 30th July the Czar declared a general mobilisation which could take up to four weeks to complete. The Austrians, whose Danube flotilla bombarded Belgrade on 29th July, ordered general mobilisation on 31st July. Germany declared war on Russia on 1st August and commenced her own mobilisation. France also began general mobilisation on 1st August. On 2nd August, Germany sent Belgium an ultimatum demanding a right of passage through Belgium. Belgium refused. On 3rd August, Germany declared war on France. On 4th August, German troops entered Belgium, as a consequence of which Britain declared war on Germany.

In summary therefore, Germany caused the First World War. She had decided to go to war between 1912-1916. She waited for an opportunity. That opportunity arose when parties working on behalf of Serb interests assassinated Austria's Archduke Ferdinand. Had Germany not supported Austria, there would have been no war. Had Austria not over-embellished the risk to the continuity of the Austro-Hungarian Empire, there would have been no war. Had Russia not backed Serbia, there might have been only a limited, local war. Had France not declared her support for Russia, there would have been no war. Had Germany not developed and carried out the Schlieffen Plan, it is possible there would have been no war, particularly one involving Britain, in which case the 11 Powerstock servicemen who did not return from war would have enjoyed normal, natural lives at home.

Richard Connaughton
Former soldier

CHAPTER 4

Lest We Forget

LEST WE FORGET: three little words murmured every Remembrance Sunday. A century on from the outbreak of the Great War, there seems little danger of forgetting the war. The government has planned a large programme of commemorative events and a veritable barrage of books and films will target every possible centenary between now and 2018. We have no chance of forgetting, but what chance we understand?

Away from the rhetoric of remembrance, the Great War is being interpreted in challenging new ways. As part of a modern 30 years' war that redrew the map of Europe. As the trigger for a succession of anti-colonial revolts, from Egypt to China, that began the rollback of centuries of Europe's global hegemony. As the start of a process of women's empowerment that was one of the great historical novelties of the 20th century. And so on.

Yet British remembrance of the Great War seems stuck in the trenches – literally and metaphorically. The period between 1914-18 evokes images of mud and blood, of young men sent to their deaths for no purpose by boneheaded, upper-class generals: the interpreters of this war experience are not historians but a few soldier poets, supremely Wilfred Owen.

There are, of course, many ways to interpret a war, and none is intrinsically right. What's interesting is why the gulf between popular stereotypes and academic perceptions of 1914-18 has become so vast.

A simple answer to the question of why the British image of the war remains stuck in the trenches might be the death toll. More than 720,000 British soldiers were killed in 1914-18 – making it the most devastating war in British military history. But around 250,000 British people died from influenza in 1918-19; the global death toll of that pandemic was somewhere between 50 and 100 million – far more than the estimated 10 million war deaths.

A better explanation may be the names of dead soldiers that are inscribed for posterity on war memorials in towns and villages across Britain and along the old Western Front in France and Belgium. This naming was novel. Most of the soldiers who died at Waterloo in 1815, like those at Agincourt in 1415, were dumped anonymously in mass graves. Only a few officers were brought home by wealthy families for decorous, personalised burial. To borrow a phrase from Shakespeare, corpses were treated 'as beseems their worth'.

This changed in the Great War. From almost the start of the conflict, bodies were collected, identified and recorded. The novelty of identity discs made this possible for the first time, but the project would not have been undertaken without the vision and drive of a now little-known journalist and educator called Fabian Ware. Too old to serve, Ware volunteered as an ambulance driver in France, where he was appalled at the random carnage and began a one-man crusade to register and tend the soldiers' graves. His legacy was the Imperial War Graves Commission, established in 1917.

All of the belligerent countries faced unprecedented challenges in dealing with mass death in the age of industrialised warfare, but the philosophy of Ware and his Commission was distinctive. They insisted that the bodies should not be brought home, mainly on grounds of cost, and they stuck to this policy even if families could afford to pay because they realised such special treatment would be deeply resented. Interestingly, the French government took a similar line but popular outcry forced it to relent and eventually nearly a third of France's identified war dead were re-interred in family graves. Most of the remainder, who had died defending their homeland, were buried on French soil.

By contrast, British Tommies were laid to rest in foreign fields, despite vociferous protest from relatives. "Many thousands of Mothers and Wives are slowly dying for want of the Grave of their loved ones to visit and tend themselves", one petition informed the Queen, "and we feel deeply hurt that the right granted to other countries is denied us".

Although statist, Ware's approach was also fundamentally democratic. Each soldier was to have his own grave, designed in a standardised way even if the family could afford something grander, and no distinction was made between a general and a private. The Commission insisted on a plain and uniform headstone rather than a Christian cross. This suited the Empire's religious diversity and

Private Richard Reed's final resting place - Bailleul Cemetery. CWGC

would be more durable against the elements, while also allowing extra room for name, rank, regiment and date of death. Next of kin were allowed to supply a short inscription but the wording was checked to avoid allowing "free scope for the effusions of the mortuary mason, the sentimental versifier, or the crank".

The apparent 'tyranny' of the War Graves Commission aroused a storm of protest. The sculptor Eric Gill called standardised headstones a 'Prussian imposition'. In parliament, Lord Robert Cecil observed that during peacetime those "closest to the deceased" were left to decide on the form of memorialisation, so why should it be any different in wartime? "Right through the Graves Commission", Cecil fumed, "is the conception of a national monument" adding that this was an "entirely novel idea". Never before had the state claimed "a right to turn the individual memorials to individual persons into a national memorial against the will and against the desire of their relatives".

But Winston Churchill, Secretary of State for War, supported the Commission in seeking to give the dead soldiers "memorials which will last for hundreds of years". It would console relatives, he declared, to know that even "the humblest soldier" would be remembered by name "through periods so remote that probably all the other memorials of this time will have faded and vanished away". This was an enduring memory of a sort previously possible only for monarchs and aristocrats.

Even where the body parts could not be identified, the remains were given dignity. Anonymous French graves bore crosses with the stark word 'Inconnu', whereas the British headstones included what details could be gleaned about rank, regiment and date of death, plus the words 'Known unto God'. This phrase was proposed by Rudyard Kipling, who also suggested the quotation 'Their Name Liveth for Evermore', from Ecclesiasticus, for the Stone of Remembrance in each cemetery.

Kipling worked indefatigably for the Commission, perhaps in expiation for his conduct during the patriotic fervour of 1914 when he pulled strings to get a commission for his acutely short-sighted son. Jack Kipling was last seen, half his face blown off, stumbling in agony on the battlefield of Loos. Like Fabian Ware, Rudyard Kipling was an old man chastened by what war had done to a younger generation, many of whom were volunteer soldiers. The continental states operated from the start with conscript armies, but Britain did not impose conscription until 1916. Some 2.5 million British men volunteered to fight, 43 per cent of those who served in the British Army in 1914-18.

The fact that millions had freely chosen to fight – including many of those who died on the Somme – left a profound impression. It certainly changed the terms of political debate, making it almost impossible by 1918 to resist demands for universal male suffrage, even for property-less workers. "What property would any man have in this country if it were not for the soldiers and sailors who are fighting our battles", declared Sir Edward Carson. "If a man is good enough to fight for you, he is good enough to vote for you."

Ware's project of war commemoration was, I think, an extension of these new wartime attitudes to democracy. Equality in death, as in life, required having a name. Hence the immense efforts undertaken to record even the names of the missing, as on the great Somme memorial at Thiepval designed by Sir Edwin Lutyens, architect of the Cenotaph.

This massive state project to give nobility and meaning to industrialised carnage resulted in nearly a thousand architect-designed cemeteries and memorials, running like a ribbon through Belgium and France. The total bill was £8.15m, about twice the cost of a single day's shelling in the last weeks of the war – burying was much cheaper than killing. But, measured against the different fiscal arithmetic of peacetime, the work of the Imperial War Graves Commission constituted one of the biggest government construction projects of the 1920s, eclipsing the modern stations of the London Underground or the programme of new telephone exchanges.

And so, on the graves in Belgium and France and on war memorials all across Britain, not to mention the walls of College chapels, these names stand out. But who were these men? What kind of people were they? Sometimes clues can be gleaned from letters home, still preserved in a family attic, or among army personnel records in the National Archives at Kew, but much is left tantalisingly to the imagination. Hence the popular appeal of war novels such as Sebastian Faulks's *Birdsong* and Pat Barker's *Regeneration Trilogy*, which try to bring the dead to life. It is perhaps the enduring presence of the names, combined with their fundamental anonymity, that makes them so arresting. So near, yet so far, and so many.

Despite all the hopes, the war of 1914-18 did not prove the war to end war. After 1945, new graves were constructed in the old way on new battlefields, at home more names were added to local war memorials, almost as a postscript. But this time victory was clear-cut and gained at roughly half the cost in British lives. This cast a different light on the conflict that had previously been known as the Great War: it became the First World War, an inconclusive precursor to the Second, which was celebrated as Britain's 'finest hour'.

Perhaps it is natural that problematic wars are memorialised in terms of cost rather than achievement. For instance, American monuments to the Second World War – which transformed the United States into a superpower – are generally heroic: a classic example is the memorial outside Washington DC, with US marines raising the stars and stripes on top of hard-won Iwo Jima. But the official memorial to the Vietnam war – which ripped cold war America apart and remains hard to justify or even explain – is simply a list of some 58,000 American dead, etched into highly reflective black stone, so that the visitor sees his or her face when tracing the name of a buddy or relative. The memorial is at once intensely abstract and yet deeply personal, the encounter of the living with the dead through the mystery of names. It is, I think, no accident that the inspiration for Maya Lin, its young Chinese-American architect, was Lutyens' Memorial to the Missing of the Somme at Thiepval.

Vietnam is still a recent scar for Americans, fifty years young, whereas all the wartime Tommies have now passed away. The soldiers of 1914 are, in fact, now as remote in time to us as they were to the Redcoats who fought Napoleon at Waterloo. The centenary of the Great War in 2014-18 is a chance to move out of the long shadows cast by those names and see the conflict in broader terms. It is time not only to remember, but also to understand.

David Reynolds

David Reynolds is Professor of International History and a Fellow of Christ's. His new book, *The Long Shadow:The Great War and the Twentieth Century,* is published by Simon & Shuster.

This article first appeared in Cambridge Alumni Magazine, Issue 70, Michaelmas 2013 and is published here with the kind permission of the Editor.

FINAL DESTINATIONS

From Powerstock to Poona
Then a single to Basra,
A sense of agriculture unfurled.
Lower Mesopotamia
Poised on the end of a bayonet.
200 rounds and a pith helmet.
Caught in the crossfire.
No more cider for George.

Poor Travers was next, Leading Stoker
Blown to smithereens off Sheerness,
Kethole Reach - Buoy 17.
Unstable, the cordite overheated,
Bulkhead near the boiler ash.
Ammunition went up. *Bulwark* vanished
In a puff of smoke - 800 others still moored
Medway between sky and water.

Fred loved chasing rabbits,
No doubt poaching was in his blood,
A bit of a lurcher or ferret still in him
As he ran off the cliff edge in Wales
At the wrong angle, gave way.
No doubt in need of some extra cash,
For beer or just the fun of it.
A gunner gone to ground. Left his post.

Sidney another gunner, C battery Field Artillery
A fishmonger's errand boy on the razzle in Egypt
Had what he thought was a touch
Of the Cairo Quickstep,

Belly ache - Belly up. Gut feeling,
Cramps his style. The burst appendix:
No match for the Pharaohs, the Sands of the Nile
The Hump on the Camel or the Sphinx's inscrutable
Smile.

Another Fred, thatching by numbers,
Took on the Turks at their own game.
Gallipoli we call it now. Landed at Anzac Cove
The heat of August, stabbing you in the back.
Only five days in the line, a Turkish bayonet
Some unnamed gully near Chunuk Bair -
Kemal's silent counter attack at dawn. Missing.
Bodies don't last long in that heat. No bones about it.

Herbert, made Sergeant, but having crossed
The salt marshes he met his end in Suvla -
On Turkish maps they call it Dragonfly Hill,
But Scimitar Hill is more precise.
A butcher no less, he sharpened his knives well
But the troops were carved up.
His cleaver put away. Ready for the chop.
Over the top. Yet another mistake.

Albert, a torpedoman at Jutland, an old salt
Aboard the *Black Prince*. But in the darkness
After Windy Corner, the armoured cruiser
Lost her way, outgunned at midnight,
Caught in German searchlights.
Point blank range, on fire from end to end,
Explodes, with all hands lost. Without a word
The North Sea opens its mouth, swallows them whole.

Charlie made Lance Corporal,
Loved the farms round Wytherston,
Delivering groceries in Barrack Street.
Any assistance required, he was there.
Bridport had its pull, as did the Western Front.

The Somme - a nice quiet sector nothing much to report.
October just the time for the apple harvest
But died of wounds all the same. Bitter fruit.

Richard, an old hand, was of an age,
When you might have thought
That war was a thing of the past.
Melplash and his forty years,
Not quite enough to save him from Flanders.
Volunteered no doubt. His wounds
Sustained near Ypres, a private matter.
A very cold day. Died three weeks later.

William, well groomed, well versed in horses,
Ended up in East Africa of all places - Z division.
A signaller in Nairobi, twiddling knobs,
Eavesdropping on the Germans. Then India beckoned.
'A gentleman of Poona would infinitely sooner'
If he could possibly help it, not contract the Spanish Flu.
Each wavelength Saps your energy below the belt.
Last month of the war. Frequency increases. Bit between
the teeth.

Harry also died abroad. A Nettlecombe man
On the China station. A stoker no less.
Made Chief Petty Officer. Oiled up.
Some run ashore, in port cruising, sailing close to the
wind
From *Carlisle* to Vladivostok, the gang plank narrow.
Shot in civilian clothes, down a remote lane.
Robbed one dark night. The subject broached,
Diamonds and rubies. Siberia. End of the Line.

© James Crowden 20th May 2014

CHAPTER 5

George Galpin
2nd Battalion The Dorsetshire Regiment
Died Sahil, Mesopotamia, 17th November 1914

GEORGE GALPIN left Powerstock to join the Dorsetshire Regiment on the 13th July 1909. He was 19 years old. He was therefore a career soldier who had found assured employment.

After working as an Agricultural Labourer over the previous six years, George would have been thrilled to be earning regular pay and receiving regular meals without being a drain on his parents. According to the 1901 census, Richard and Mary had five children, Henry, George, Arthur, Joseph and Charles although there was Florence who was six in the 1891 census, which one can only assume was an adoption or assistance to someone who had a baby out of wedlock. Charles became a carpenter like his father and worked in Powerstock for Leaf Brothers (still going today) and created the wooden memorial to the soldiers of Powerstock. This historical relic has been the subject of a detailed search but has not been located. The Galpins had been around the Bridport area for a few hundred years. There is a memorial in the grounds of St Mary's Church, Bridport beginning with Richard Galpin in June 1760 through to Mary Galpin who died in 1837.

George might have been thinking about enlisting for a good while since he could have hitched a lift on a cart or gone to Dorchester market for his employer on occasions and the seed of the idea may have grown in his mind. He would have been able to chat to soldiers in the town to find out about life in the Army as well as life outside the area.

The Regiment would have been very pleased to recruit a young man such as George. He was very fit and stood at nearly 6'1" (the average height was then 5'6"). His Soldiers' Book adds that he had a fresh complexion, brown eyes and hair with, incidentally, the distinguishing mark of three scars below his right nipple. George's book indicates he joined at the unlikely age of 19 years and 9 months, which means he would have been born within three months of his elder brother Richard. We have to assume he was probably 19 years old or younger. The 1911 Census gave the Galpin parents as having a mere two dependants although there were originally six, all of whom were still alive at that time.

For six weeks, no recruit was allowed out of barracks as it was considered undesirable to allow them to go home during that period – it was a tough induction and since they had never been away from home, they might be homesick. After his initial three months training, during which there is no leave, it would have been a relief for George to enjoy going home to Powerstock for a drink in The Three Horseshoes and enjoy a social life outside barracks, but he was posted to Portsmouth on the 5th October 1910 and eleven days later, 8740 Private George Galpin was shipped out to Poona (Pune), India, to join the 2nd Battalion The Dorsetshire Regiment. Poona was the largest garrison of the Raj.

Poona is a hilly area, the tallest hill 2,600 feet, and is cooler than most of India. It has three seasons, summer, monsoon and winter. The winter is a pleasant temperature ranging from 10°C-28°C. From 1875 until 1910, the city was a major centre of agitation including demands for independence from Britain. Understandably, any regiment stationed there would have been required to be well practised at Keeping the Peace.

It is strange that the Dorset Regiment had a motto that boasts of being the first in India, for being in India was antisocial to say the least. All personnel in a Battalion, on a tour to India, would have known that they were going to be there for 3-4 years or longer. The logistics could not allow a short posting and as a result they would establish their own communities within the Empire.

The daily routine was just that: Reveille 06:30, Roll Call, Breakfast, Drill, PT (Swedish Drill – brought in following the humiliation of the British Army by a group of Dutch settlers during the Boer War, after which the Generals and Politicians decided to blame the soldiers' lack of fitness and instituted a regime of exercise), Training, Lunch for officers and Dinner for men, Training, Sport on Wednesdays, Pay Parade on Thursdays, Tea, Supper, Lights out 22:00.

Within the battalion, there would have been their own Tailor, Carpenter, Smith, Printer, Armourer, Sign Writer – all carrying out their trades as in a small town, which is what their barracks became. They would have been encouraged to join a temperance movement to prevent drunkenness – whatever a squaddie can bring to that. The officers and some warrant officers may well have been accompanied by their wives. The officers' wives tended to form their own social circle.

The Medical Officer did his best to treat tropical diseases unknown to him at home. He had the support of a military hospital. Poona had had an outbreak of plague ten years before the Battalion arrived. The men lived in airy barrack rooms which they soon filled with pipe and baccy smoke. They employed punka-wallahs to fan the rooms and had char(tea)-wallahs, and dhobi-wallahs to do their washing. It was also not unusual to have somebody shave them, so the soldiers got to know a small part of the local community through their daily lives. Poona had a thriving market which the Quartermaster dealt with to procure fresh rations. Presumably the Army's staple meat, bully beef, had to be controlled for fear of creating offence among the local community.

It was the norm for units to rotate from the cool hills in summer back to the plains in winter and there would be periods of acclimatisation when they went on route marches for exercise and 'showing the flag'. Sport and hunting would have played a large part in the recreation and entertainment of the officers.

The done thing was for leave to be taken locally, to let one's hair down away from the barrack town. A squaddie in the early 20th century was not well educated and often undertook basic Part 3 Education which provided him with a standard of numeracy and literacy. Part 3 Education was the first step in qualifying for promotion. Parts 2 and 1 were required for promotion to higher ranks. George passed his Part 3 in March 1912. His letters were definitely written in his own hand but his signature in his Soldiers' Book is an over-write so one must assume that the writing improved with his Army education.

On the 21st November 1913, George wrote from Poona to his brother Richard or Dick, or Henry as the census has him, who had recently joined the Army (Royal Engineers and subsequently won the Military Medal for "his bravery and determination in executing his duties under heavy fire near Moyenneville on 21st August 1918"), whose most welcoming son Brian lives in Manor Fields,

Bridport. Brian has supplied much invaluable information including the following letter from George in India to elder brother Dick who had recently joined the army:

Dear Brother

I hope this few lines will find you in the very best of health as I am very pleased to say it leaves me so.

Well Dick, what do you think of life after being in the Army? I don't suppose you can recommend it. I am very pleased to hear that you have obtained some work and I hope it will last out for it ain't much cop to be with-out work but I did not expect you to stop at home. I fully expected to hear that you was in the police or some-thing of that sort but of course not everybody is of the same opinion. How do you find the English beer? I suppose you have tested it long enough before now. Roll on Dick when I hope we shall have a drink together once more, although I can honestly say that it is nearly three years ago now that a drop of beer or any intoxicating licquor passed my lips, and I hope please God to be able to say the same thing when I come home for I don't intend to touch another drop in India but I hope by the time I come home to have a tidy little Bank Book for I am saving rather more than a pound a month.

Well Dick I can't stop any longer this time but will write more next time so must close I remain,

Yours

Loving Brother, George

I don't suppose Dick you have a photo anywhere at all as I should very much like one.

Back with the regiment in India, the specialist soldiers, such as Signallers and Machine gunners would regularly practice and aim for higher trade efficiency which carried greater pay.

If the soldier survived, he would have had a character building exercise for life as well as a financial bonus. The down side could be coming back home crippled with alcoholism, pox and malaria. The shock of being in a place such as India, to a British soldier, would have been immense. The climate, the currency and the fact that cows were venerated, were all startlingly different, as was the already mentioned fact that the common soldier had people to wait on him.

So this was the life George Galpin was living in India, but from his Soldiers' Small Book, we see that he obtained two good conduct badges in July 1911 and 1914, as well as a swimming proficiency badge in April 1911. George's Musketry Qualifications were outstanding as he obtained a First in 1911, 1912 and 1913. The Small Book is not only a record of personal achievement but also acts as an aide memoire on the nitty gritty of army life including: how to salute, rifle cleaning, cleaning clothes, points to note when on guard or at outposts, how to prevent sore feet, notes on field cooking and hints for the preparation of food, furloughs, marriage and civil employment.

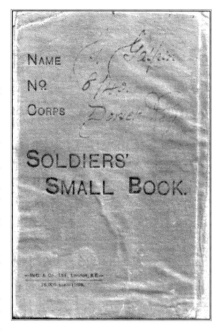

These successes would have earned him extra pay, although George went the way of many a soldier who enjoyed the fleshpots of Poona and ended up in hospital in January and February 1914 for 32 days with venereal disease. His proficiency pay was stopped because he had 'rendered himself unfit for duty'. In August, he was in hospital again for a week, this time with malaria.

During his time in India, the map of Europe was about to change forever as events eventually overtook each other to plunge the world into war. At which point did George Galpin and his fellow soldiers receive information which might have leaked down from officers aware of what was happening in Europe? It was probably only taken seriously when they began two months of intensive training from mid August, after which they might have expected to be sent there.

George Galpin was the first of the 11 of the Parish to die. His garrison town was Poona and ironically it was to Poona that the last of our fallen came to die before the Armistice. There is a sense of how small the cogs were as represented by the men of the 2nd

Dorsets compared to the large cogs in a Grand Design in which they featured.

The 16th (Poona) Brigade, part of the 6th Indian (Poona) Division (Plate 5) commanded by Major-General Charles Townshend, embarked on the 18th October 1914. There had been no mention of their ultimate destination although the issue of pith helmets strongly suggested they were not going to Europe. George Galpin and the other representatives of the parishes of Dorset operated at the tactical level of war in sections and platoons. On the broader canvas there was a strategic rationale for what they were about to do and a grand strategy above that. On 23rd October, the Indian Army forces that had been sent originally as contingency forces to Bahrain to protect the oil refineries, waited for a declaration of war before commencing an invasion of southern Mesopotamia. Originally, operations in Mesopotamia were the responsibility of the Indian Army, until the War Office took over.

It had been a correct assumption that oil had been a rationale for the invasion of Mesopotamia (Iraq). Super dreadnoughts were now powered by oil-fired turbines. The worldwide network of coaling stations, brim full with Welsh anthracite, of which Britain then had inexhaustible stocks, became obsolescent to oil, of which Britain had none of its own. As a contingency, Britain took a controlling interest in the Anglo-Persia (Iran) Oil Company. The oil flowed through a pipeline to Abadan on the Shatt al-Arab estuary of the rivers Tigris and Euphrates where it was refined. Overlooked by Turkish Mesopotamia, there was a possibility of supply being cut off in the event of war. In 1883, the Ottomans sought German assistance to reorganise their army, a measure widely viewed as an important part of *'Drang nach Osten'* or 'Thrust towards the East', motivated by the Kaiser's desire for new lands and markets at the expense of Britain and France.

Much of India's army had been committed to Europe, apparently with the gratifying support of her people, but she had no naval resources to speak of. If forces were to operate in Mesopotamia, they would need waterborne transport for the rivers Tigris and Euphrates which were the main communication routes across the country. The Royal Navy supplied shallow-draught vessels brought in from China and East Africa which were to supply gunfire support to the army in its advance up the Tigris.

This diversion of the Indian Expeditionary Force (IEF), as it became known, to the Persian Gulf came into being because, in addition to protecting the oil refineries at Abadan, control of Mesopotamia and the wider Middle East afforded easier access not only to Afghanistan and Persia, but also to Egypt and the Suez Canal. The Indian government's orders to the British regional Commander-in-Chief included a provision that allowed him to attack the Turk-controlled port of Basra should formal hostilities break out between Britain and Turkey. While the London War Office was in favour of a cautious strategy of simply defending British oil supplies in Mesopotamia, the Indian government advocated a policy of so-called 'forward defence'. It would appear that London's Arabist Foreign Office harboured a wider intention than the War Office.

The 16th Infantry Brigade (2nd Dorsetshire Regt, 104th Wellesley's Rifles, 117th Mahrattas and the 20th DCO Infantry (Brownlow's Punjabis) and the 1st Indian Mountain Artillery Brigade (23rd and 30th Indian Mountain Artillery Batteries) – a total of 4731 officers and men, embarked at Bombay in a convoy totalling 54 ships. They set sail for Mesopotamia on the 18th of October under the command of Brigadier-General W.S. Delamain. Amongst them, George Galpin was one of the 2nd Battalion's 869 other ranks. There were also five warrant officers and 22 officers, amongst whom would have been one Captain Frank Middleton, son of the squire of nearby Dorset village Bradford Peverell on board their heavy transport ship, *HT Varela*, a British-India liner. This was the advanced striking force of Expeditionary Force 'D'. Brigadier Delamain's instructions were to occupy Abadan Island in order to protect the oil refineries there, cover the landing of reinforcements, and assure local Arabs of British support for them against the Turks. Although the Persians remained generally favourable towards the British and the Arab Sheiks including Kuwait, the Arab tribes of coastal Mesopotamia often changed sides.

Varela arrived in Bahrain on October 23rd. The British forces were told to delay disembarkation, waiting in extremely hot conditions on board their ships until such time as the Turks entered the war, which they did on November 2nd after the Turks had assisted Germany on 29th October in a naval bombardment of the Russian Black Sea coast. The principal ships had been the erstwhile German *Göeben* and *Breslau*. Russia declared war on Turkey, followed by

Britain's declaration against Turkey on 5th November. The Turkish alignment with Germany closed the Dardanelles to the allies.

The *Varela* sailed to Kharag Island, Persia, and there then followed the first action of the Mesopotamian campaign which was the taking of the fort at Fao Landing, a mere 10 hours away, on November 6th .

Some 600 British troops, including a contingent of the Dorsets, landed near the old fort but the rest of the force sailed on to a place where they could safely disembark. Assuming George was in that first detachment, he and his fellow soldiers would have had a hard time landing as there were no barges, tugs or suitable small boats and the land transport was poor. On arrival at the beach, they were met with heavy fire from Fao fortress in addition to gunfire from the mouth of the Tigris. As the British advanced, they were met with Ottoman infantry assaults, which they managed to repel but they could not take the fortress because their heavy artillery had not yet landed. They dug trenches around the Fortress and exchanged occasional fire.

When the heavy artillery arrived, the British immediately began bombarding the Ottoman fort. The walls were fairly soon breached and the British charged into the fortress where the two sides fought for their lives at close quarters. The fort and 300 Ottoman prisoners were captured and the British marched into the port of Fao the next day, when the rest of the division began landing.

With Fao captured, the Ottomans no longer controlled any part of the Persian Gulf. The British facilities were technically safe. However, the British felt that their facilities would not be truly safe until they managed to capture Baghdad, which meant going forward to Basra, 60 miles away, covering the same ground as that captured by British Forces in the 2003 Iraq War.

Reaching Abadan on November 7th, the British force defeated some light Turkish resistance before establishing a fortified camp some three miles further up the river, after which, on November 11th, an attack was launched by 400 Turkish troops, which was repulsed with heavy loss and the Turks withdrew some four miles. Within a further three days, Expeditionary Force D had been reinforced with a much-needed additional 7000 Indian troops, along with light artillery. The next day, a British reconnaissance force inflicted further losses on the Turks near Saihan. Conditions were poor, with thick dust, mud and heat mirage. On the same day, the remainder of the Poona Division landed.

On November 15th, British troops including the 2nd Battalion The Dorset Regiment advanced further up the Tigris and confronted a 3000-strong Turkish force at Saihan. The conditions were now awful with a mix of thick dust and heat as well as heavy rainfall and mud (Plate 6). Their progress was slow until the 18-pounder artillery succeeded in forcing the enemy to retreat. There were 60 casualties suffered, of which two-thirds were from the 2nd Dorsets, giving a fair indication of their important role in the battle.

George wrote to his mother the next day, his address as from India, and his letter is reproduced verbatim:

Mrs R. Galpin, Powerstock, Melplash, Dorset England.
8740, Pte G Galpin, H Coy 2nd Dorsets, 6th Poona Division,
16th Infantry Brigade, C/O Postmaster Gen, Bombay, India.

Dear Mother and all at home,

I hope these few lines will find you in the very best of health, as I am very pleased to be able to say it leaves me so. I hope you received the photoes alright, I cant promis when I shall be able to write again so if you dont get a letter for a few months, dont get worring over it. I suppose you have seen all about us leaving Bombay and all the news about how we have been getting on, that is the best thing to do is to follow up the papers and I expect you will see if anything should happen. You must please excuse this scribble as I am writing it in a very funny position and I may say I haven't had a wash or a shave for nearly a fortnight. Cant stop any longer so buck up please remember me to all so must close.
With love to all from
Yours Alway Loving Son, George xxx

The next morning, November 17th at 06.00, the 18th Brigade, followed by George's 16th Brigade, moved North to Sahil. A report of the day's proceedings from a senior officer stated that no baggage was allowed and all ranks carried only great coats, 200 rounds of ammunition and 24 hours worth of cooked rations. The going was very wet and heavy which was distressing to the men and horses.

Firing started from the fort at 10.10 and shortly afterwards the 16th Brigade was ordered to close up and formed up some three miles south west of the Old Fort. Information regarding the enemy was sketchy and what was thought to be was not correct, as the enemy's forces extended much further north than was understood.

At 10.35, the Dorsets were allotted to a frontal attack south of the Old Fort. On George's left, the 20th Punjabis extended the northerly line. Both the Dorsets and the 20th were ordered to march on the south-western corner of the Old Fort. From the start, the heavy rain and mist rendered the Old Fort invisible for much of the time. About 1000 yards from the Old Fort, the enemy suddenly opened a heavy fire.

It then became apparent that the Turks' left flank did not stop at the Old Fort but extended in a southerly direction along a series of mounds and banks along the edge of the date palms, while it extended on the other flank in a north-westerly direction. The Dorsets were thus under a crossfire and there were many casualties including the deaths of Major Mercer and, 400 yards from the Fort, Captain Middleton (from Bradford Peverell) as well as other ranks who are not mentioned by name.

It is fairly certain that this is where Powerstock's own George Galpin will have fallen, just a day after that poignant letter to his family which has GG, 16.11.14 written on the seal of the envelope. The letter was posted with the stamp of the IEF and is likely to have arrived in Powerstock after Mary and Richard Galpin had received the news of George's death (Plate 7). They might have taken some solace from the fact that there was no sign of apprehension in the letter and that he almost took some pride in the fact that he had not shaved or washed since he and his mates had arrived at Fao on November 6th. It is a letter from a loving son who is doing his job and seemingly not thinking too much about the dangers that lay ahead. The action continued and, on the right flank, a jammed machine gun was taken up and repaired by a Private Hughes after his Lieutenant was killed. Under heavy fire, he brought it to close range and made very good use of it.

On the left, where George undoubtedly lay, they had a worse time and were unable to progress so fast but at about 12.55 when the right of the Battalion arrived approximately 300 yards from the date palms, the reserve battalions were brought up on its right. They were thrown into the firing line and this resulted in a movement led by Lieutenant Stephenson to whom command had devolved on the death of his Major and Captain. He led the Dorsets into the date palms and together with the Brigade Reserves swept northwards, inflicting heavy loss on the enemy en route.

As the remainder of the Battalion advanced on the Fort by rushes, the Turks fled. The Fort was captured at 13.30 and the enemy's whole line retired, often using heat mirages as cover but, with conditions being so muddy, the British were unable to give chase.

High winds caused several supply barges to break their moorings while some sank and others ran aground. The resulting loss of rations forced the troops to kill and eat the wounded Arab ponies that the Turkish forces had left behind. In this battle, the 2nd Dorsets again contributed disproportionately to the 500 or so British casualties, with 22 killed and 149 wounded. These heavy casualties were caused partially by the fact that the attack was made over ground as flat as a billiard table, partially by the crossfire and partially by the entire absence of Artillery support. It had only been two weeks since their arrival and they had already had 25 per cent of their force put out of action.

The Battalion re-formed in the Old Fort and advanced to the enemy's camp some two miles north of the Fort. The camp was partially burnt and some ammunition thrown into the canal but owing to the lateness of the hour, the Battalion had to return to its bivouac before the work was completed. The bivouac was just two miles south of the Fort. The Battalion arrived there just as it was getting dark at about 17.00, and in a blinding sandstorm.

Later in the evening, Lieutenant General Sir A. Barrett, force commander, came round to the bivouac area and congratulated the Battalion on its conduct during the fight.

Shortly after his death, George Galpin's body was removed to the Commonwealth War Grave Cemetery in Basra, occupied on 22nd November. During the course of the recent Iraq conflicts, the cemetery was progressively destroyed. Every one of the 4000 headstones had been vandalised by local people. The Roll of Honour is available to be seen at the War Graves' HQ in Maidenhead.

Like all soldiers' families, the Galpin family had to suffer the heartbreak of dealing with George's effects as well as impersonal letters from the War Office. These required his father repeatedly filling in details of George's death as acknowledgement for receiving the balance of his estate and providing proof for the sending of the 1914 Star and the Victory and War Medals – Pip, Squeak and Wilfred.

The Galpin family did their bit as Arthur was in the Royal Garrison Artillery in France, Joseph was in the Royal Field Artillery in India, Richard was in the Royal Engineers and Charlie was also in the army. Charlie was married in 1932 and there is a picture of his wedding party outside Southover House in Nettlecombe with the smallest girl at the front named Betty Bull who has been immensely helpful with the social history of the village. Richard was married in Powerstock in February 1930.

After this beginning against the forces of the Ottoman Empire and despite the Dorsets, in particular, losing a disproportionate number of men, it was an over-confident and under-resourced British campaign buoyed by early and misleadingly easy victories. The British suffered stinging losses, particularly after they were besieged further up river at Kut-al-Amara. This led to the worst military defeat of the campaign the British force had suffered. On 29th April 1916, General Townshend and 13,000 men, including the 2nd Dorsets, surrendered. The subsequent treatment of the POWs by Turkish troops on their long march to Turkey and later employed in heavy work duties was nothing short of barbaric and was considered controversial even to the Turks' German allies. The British campaign after the disaster of Kut benefited from considerably greater supplies of men and equipment, allowing them to outnumber the Ottoman forces while enjoying the advantage of superior armaments. Two years later the Ottoman Empire lay in ruins.

It will have been pleasing for a Galpin family friend, Harry Gale, to join the Mesopotamian Expeditionary Force in 1917 as they heaped revenge on the Turks and swept them away with their considerably superior support. He and George Galpin were part of a little known campaign (as far as the public at home were aware) which, although not in the forefront of people's minds and not on Britain's doorstep, was nevertheless immensely important.

In all, George Galpin's time in the 2nd Dorsets consisted of one year and four days at home; four years 32 days in India; 12 days in Mesopotamia. A total of five years and 128 days, another tragedy in the annals of a war when so many young men died.

International relations between London and Paris at the time were emblematic of an attitude apparent in the Peloponnesian Wars that the strong take what they will, the weak suffer as they must. Britain had secured its objective of protecting its oil supply. The reason they did not stop there was in order to inherit the possessions of Turkey, 'the sick man of Europe'. This aspiration led to the Sykes-Picot agreement apportioning the Turkish territories between Britain and France and excluding Germany. The Balfour Agreement promising the Jewish people Palestine as a national home, nevertheless envisaged Britain as the keyholder of that particular door. How else could the rights of the then 90 per cent Arab population of Palestine be protected? By themselves, the words in the Declaration would be an insufficient safeguard: "nothing shall be done which may prejudice the civil and religious rights of existing non-Jewish communities". Almost all of today's problems in the Middle East can be attributed to this example of colonial Grand Strategy. Little did young George Galpin realise that he was a minute, disposable instrument of such an aspiration.

The British Army had failed twice in South Africa and failed in the centrepiece of the Mesopotamian Front due to General Nixon in Basra having no feel for the capabilities of men in protracted combat at the end of an over-extended supply line. Gallipoli was a humiliating disaster. The British failed in Basra in 2007 trying to control a city of one million people with three battalions, which had reduced to one by 2007. When we look at what we ask our Galpins to do, it matters not how good they undoubtedly are, for that in itself will never overcome a lack of political will or the poverty of Generalship.

Jamie Turner
Musician

CHAPTER 6

Frederick Hubert Reginald Travers
HMS Bulwark
Died Sheerness, 26th November 1914

FREDERICK HUBERT Reginald Travers was born on 22nd September 1889, the eldest son of Ernest Edgar Travers and his wife Mary Ann Elizabeth, née Harris. He was baptised in Loders Church on 27th October 1889. His father was an Agricultural Labourer, born in Uploders on 23rd August 1864 and when he died in 1910 aged 46 he had been living in Nettlecombe. His mother was born and baptised in Bridport in 1868 and Fred's parents were married in 1886. They produced four daughters and four sons; one of the latter died aged 3. Mary Ann died in Melplash in September 1908, aged 41. Ernest's family tree was brought to my attention by a distant cousin, Geraldine Gasparelli.

Very little is known of Fred's early life. The census of 1901 shows that he went to school and it is assumed that the school would have been Loders School. He followed his father in becoming an Agricultural Labourer. It was probably on joining the Royal Navy that he nominated his sister Myrtle (then aged 6) as his Next-of-Kin. She died in 1992 but we have obtained through an acquaintance of hers some photographs almost certainly of Fred in his early twenties.

Aged 20, Fred joined the Royal Navy on 15th April 1910 as a Stoker 2nd Class on a 12 year engagement, with Service Number K 6012. On entry he was described as 5 feet 6½ inches in height, with a chest of 35½ inches, having brown hair, grey eyes and a fair complexion. There was a mark on his right hip.

He started his initial training when ordered to report to *HMS Victory II*, which was the ship's name for the Royal Naval Barracks at Portsmouth, giving new recruits shore-based training. After three weeks of learning how to wear his uniform and how to march and keep a tidy kit he was drafted to *HMS Renown*, his first sea-going ship, on 8th May 1910.

Plates 1 & 2.
Powerstock, Dorset
at the beginning of
the 20th Century.

Plate 3. Nettlecombe's ham stone terraced cottages circa 1698. The left hand cottage, Stones Cottage, was the home of William Stone's father and stepmother, also his aunt.

© *Megan Poole*

Plate 4.
Heir to the Austro-Hungarian throne Archduke Franz Ferdinand and his wife, Sophie, get into a motor car to depart from the City Hall, Sarajevo, shortly before they were assassinated by the nationalist Gavrilo Princip on 28 June 1914.
IWM (Q81831)

Plate 5. Indian troops embarking horses at Bombay.
© *The Keep Military Museum, Dorchester*

Plate 6. Dorsets advancing near Basra mostly through flooded roads in November 1914.
© *The Keep Military Museum, Dorchester*

Plate 7.
Local Roll of Honour. Pte G.
Galpin, first left.
Western Gazette,
Friday, February 5, 1915.

"Dulce et Decorum est pro Patria Mori."

OUR LOCAL ROLL OF HONOUR.

AMONG THE KILLED AND WOUNDED.

Priv. G. Galpin, (3d Dorset, Powerstock, Killed, Persian Gulf. — Priv. W. Pu´ge, (Scots Guards), Child Okeford. Killed. — Drummer E. A. Ford, (1st Wilts), Normanton. Wounded. — Priv. J. Buss, (1st Hants), Breamore. Wounded. — Lance-Corpl. N. Fry, (Canadian L.I.), Wilton. Killed.

Plate 8. *HMS Bulwark*, a 15,000 ton pre-dreadnought, blew up at Sheerness,
26 November 1914. Of the complement of 750, no officers and only 14 ratings survived.
Illustrated War News, Part 17, December 2nd 1914.

Plate 9.
One apparent naval
architectural problem
lay in piles of hot
ash and ammunition
magazines sharing
the other side of the
same wall.

Plate 10. A battleship munitioning.

Plate 11. Frederick Travers.

Plate 12. West Blockhouse, Angle, South Wales.
6 inch & 9.2 inch gun emplacements 1938.
Late James Eaton-Evans via Roger J.C. Thomas

Plate 13. At sea level, the site of East Blockhouse and the feed position of the anti-submarine boom. The Robson home, on the cliff top from which at some point Gunner Fred Symes fell to his death.

© *Jennie and Simon Robson*

Plate 14. Fred Symes' grave, Church of St Mary, Angle, Pembrokeshire.

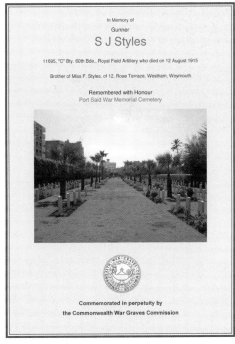

Plate 15. The inscription on Sidney Styles' headstone in the Port Said Cemetery reads 'brother of Miss F. Styles of Weymouth' and the address given for Fanny is the family home, where his parents and other siblings were still living.

Plate 16
Sidney Styles' childhood home,
12 Rose Terrace (later Granville Road)
Weymouth.

Plate 17
Tidings Wanted. The second name is that of Biles, Private F.G., 10303, D Company, 10th Hampshire Regiment. Hope springs eternal for parents in search of their sons. Fred Biles had been dead for over three months.
Western Gazette,
Friday 19 November 1915

Plates 18 and 19.
British troops August & September 1915.
There is an impression arising from Gallipoli, how the number of casualties might have been significantly reduced for want of better dispersal. We see this in ship to shore movement and in the attack where the enemy made good use of artillery and machine guns. We were too obliging in our presentation of quality targets.
The problem in such an observation is answered in Plate 20. When the troops do take cover, they cannot progress.

Plates 19 & 20
Gallipoli. British Troops
August and September
1915.

Plate 21
No.4 Troop,
A Squadron,
commanded by
Douglas Pass.
One of the two
sergeants is
probably Fred
Hansford.
Photo postcard
of the Dorset
Yeomanry during
First World War -
Facebook.

Plate 22. Colonel Troyte Bullock who commanded the Dorset Yeomanry attack on Scimitar Hill. © *The Keep Military Museum, Dorchester*

Plate 23. Albert Tiltman. A coloured photograph in the possession of his granddaughter, Diana Wells.

Plate 24. *HMS Espiegle*, from a photograph in the possession of Mr J.J. Heath-Caldwell. Albert Tiltman served in *HMS Espiegle* before the war. She and her sister ship *HMS Clio* were in action in the Mesopotamia campaign. *HMS Espiegle* was the last of HM Ships to carry a figurehead, a green-haired (it was the fashion then) woman.

HMS Renown was a second-class pre-dreadnought battleship built at Pembroke Dockyard (near Milford Haven) for the Royal Navy between 1893 and 1897. She was 412 feet 3 inches long and had a beam of 72 feet 4 inches and her draught was 27 feet 3 inches. She displaced about 13,000 tons. She was powered by two three-cylinder vertical triple expansion steam engines each driving a single propeller. Steam was provided by eight cylindrical boilers with a working pressure of 155 psi. Although she was designed to reach a speed of 17 knots her engines proved to be more powerful than anticipated and she reached 18.75 knots during her sea trials. The ship carried a maximum of 1890 tons of coal, enough to steam 6400 nautical miles at 10 knots. Her main armament was four 40-calibre, breech loading 10-inch Mk III guns. Her complement was around 655.

HMS Renown was nicknamed the 'Battleship Yacht'. Intended to command cruiser squadrons operating out of foreign stations she served as flagship for the Commander-in-Chief at the Fleet Review at Spithead in the June 1897 Diamond Jubilee of Queen Victoria. Then she became Admiral 'Jackie' Fisher's flagship on the North America and West Indies Station and later his flagship of the Mediterranean Fleet. In 1902 she had carried the Duke and Duchess of Connaught on a royal tour of India and in 1905 the Prince and Princess of Wales – the future King George V and Queen Mary – embarked for another royal tour of India. In 1907 *Renown* carried King Alfonso XIII and Queen Victoria Eugenia of Spain on an official trip to and from the United Kingdom. In between all these events the ship had participated in many combined manoeuvres. At the end of 1909 she was converted for use as a stoker's training ship. I give these details as Stoker 2nd Class Travers served for two months on board, learning the ins and outs of his job, almost certainly in the engine and boiler rooms.

Please do not think that life in HM Ships in those days was easy. In his book *The Great War at Sea (1914-1918)* Richard Hough tells us that conditions of service at the time were tough. "Just one penny" he wrote "had been added to the pay of 1s 7d a day granted in 1852, the food was at the best basic, and the system of maintaining discipline was petty and undignified. Winston Churchill, First Lord of the Admiralty, made some reforms in 1912 and these did away with many injustices and led to higher pay and more generous leave, and restrictions on the powers of the ships' police." Fred would have had the problem of overcoming sea-sickness, quite often brought about by the smells and fumes encountered in the course of a stoker's work.

(Writing about this aspect of life in a warship and at sea has brought back to me memories of 1950 and my first time onboard two of His Majesty's Ships, when as a Combined Cadet Force (CCF) cadet at my school, aged 15, I spent a week living in the Boys' Mess of the Cruiser HMS Cleopatra alongside in Chatham and then the next week at sea onboard the Minesweeper HMS Romola sailing from Fishguard to Plymouth.

Slinging my hammock in the Boys' Mess of Cleopatra was a new experience but when I got into it I stared at the deckhead (ceiling) to see about a thousand cockroaches moving about above me with the occasional one or two dropping onto me. Romola was a small ship and she was tossed around in heavy seas. I had not 'found my sealegs' and the movement and the smell of Furnace Fuel Oil made me very sick. I recall when we were off St Ives being sent for and told a telegram had been received from my parents "Have you tried Quells?")

Fred Travers would by now have become accustomed to many of the tribulations of service in the Royal Navy. He would have been a proficient junior stoker and ready to join an operational ship. So he went back to *Victory II* for some leave and joined his next ship, *HMS Albemarle*, on 24th August 1910.

HMS Albemarle was a pre-dreadnought Duncan-class battleship built at Chatham Dockyard between January 1900 and November 1903. She was 432 feet long, had a beam of 75 feet 6 inches and a draught of 25 feet 9 inches. She displaced 13,270 tons at normal load. She was powered by 4-cylinder triple expansion engines. Steam was provided by 24 Belleville water tube boilers. She had two shafts. Her designed speed was 19 knots and she had a range of 7000 nautical miles at 10 knots. Her main armament was four 40-calibre, breech loading 12-inch Mk IX guns. Her complement was 720.

When Stoker Travers was a member of her ship's company the ship was part of the Third Division of the Home Fleet based in Portsmouth. She went on to serve in the First World War in the Channel Fleet and for some of the time was based at Portland. In

November 1915 she was ordered to move to the Mediterranean. She left Scapa Flow with three other battleships but encountered extremely heavy weather in the Pentland Firth and suffered severe damage when two large waves struck in rapid succession, wrecking her bridge and charthouse and flooding her forward main gun turret, mess decks and flats. There were losses of life and serious injuries. After repairs, in January 1916 she served in North Russia as guard ship and icebreaker and flagship for Senior Naval Officer, Murmansk.

Stoker Travers left her on 14th December 1910 and was drafted to *HMS Prince of Wales*; he would serve in her until 12th May 1912. On 15th April 1911, having been a Stoker 2nd Class since joining the RN, he was rated up to Stoker 1st Class after one year in the Navy. The qualifications he required to pass as a Stoker 1st Class were:

- Efficiency as a fireman when boiler is working at full power.
- Ability to attend and lubricate a bearing.
- Knowledge of the names and uses of the principal tools in ordinary use in the Engine-room Department.
- An intelligent use of the more simple ones, e.g., spanner, hammer and chisel, file, screw-driver.
- Ability to plait gasket for packing.
- A fair knowledge of the Stokers' Manual.

The examination will be conducted by the Engineer Officer of the ship. (*In addition a fair knowledge of Rifle Exercises will be required*)

HMS Prince of Wales was a London- or Queen-class (or sometimes known as the Formidable class) pre-dreadnought battleship, the sixth in the line of ships of the Royal Navy with that name. She was built in Chatham Dockyard between March 1901 and May 1904. She was 431 feet 9 inches long, had a beam of 75 feet and a draught of 25 feet 4 inches. She displaced approximately 15,000 tons. Her power came from two vertical triple expansion engines driving two shafts and her boilers were of the water tube type. Her speed was 18 knots and she had a range of 5500 nautical miles at 10 knots. Her main armament consisted of four 40-calibre, breech loading 12-inch Mk IX guns. Her complement was 747.

Small details of her time in service are that in 1904 she was in the Mediterranean Fleet. She had a minor collision with a merchant steamer *SS Enidiven* in 1905 and in 1906 she had a fatal accident when she suffered a machinery explosion during high speed trials; three men were killed and four injured. When Fred Travers was on board *HMS Prince of Wales* (14/12/10 to 12/5/12) the ship had transferred to the Atlantic Fleet and was Flagship to a Vice Admiral. In 1911 she underwent a refit in Gibraltar so Fred would have had the experience of the Mediterranean climate and the pleasures of Main Street, Gibraltar.

Fred Travers joined *HMS Bulwark* on 30th June 1912. This ship belonged, like his previous one, to the Formidable- or London-class of pre-dreadnought battleships. She was built at Devonport Dockyard between 1899 and 1902. She had the same dimensions and characteristics as Travers's previous ship so he should have been familiar with the machinery. She had a main armament of four 40-calibre, breech-loading 12-inch guns. The ship saw early service in her life as part of the Mediterranean Fleet, relieving Travers's first ship *Renown* as the fleet flagship. In 1907 she joined the Home Fleet as Flagship of the Nore Division. Her Commander in 1908 had been Captain Robert Falcon Scott of Antarctic fame, the youngest battleship commander at that time. After a refit in 1911 she grounded twice on Barrow Deep off the Nore during sea trials, suffering some bottom damage in May 1912. With the refit complete in June 1912 (the month that Travers joined her) she became a unit of the Fifth Battle Squadron.

On 14th April 1913 Fred Travers was awarded his first Good Conduct badge. On 23rd August 1914 he was rated up to Acting Leading Stoker. His story would not be complete if I didn't state what his qualifications now had to be:

- To be of two years' service as Stoker 1st Class, and not within two years of completing the first period of service.
- To be a specially selected Stoker 1st Class on board a seagoing ship, and to have undergone satisfactorily a course of watch-keeping at all classes of auxiliary machinery in the ship.
- To show a fair knowledge of one of the following trades: Fitter and Turner, Boilermaker and Smith, Coppersmith, Moulder.
- Must have a knowledge of and be able to work simple examples

in the first four rules of arithmetic, do simple sums in money involving addition and subtraction only, and be able to read and write fairly.

From the beginning of the First World War on 4th August 1914, *Bulwark* and the Fifth Battle Squadron, assigned to the Channel Fleet and based at Portland, carried out numerous patrols in the English Channel under the command of Captain Guy Sclater.

From 5th to 9th November, while anchored at Portland, *Bulwark* 'hosted' the Court Martial of Rear-Admiral Sir Ernest Charles Thomas Troubridge for his actions during the pursuit of the German battlecruiser *SMS Göben* and the light cruiser *SMS Breslau* in the Mediterranean Sea in August 1914. *(Because this was one of the earliest actions of the war and contemporaneous with Travers's naval career, the reasons for this court martial appear later in this chapter. As will be seen, the failure of the Royal Navy to properly engage the German ships allowed those ships to influence naval operations in the Black Sea for many years. It also had an unfortunate effect at Gallipoli.)*

On 14th November 1914, the Fifth Battle Squadron transferred to Sheerness to guard against a possible German invasion of England.

We now come to the death of *HMS Bulwark* and almost all of her ship's company. When she reached the River Medway, *Bulwark* was moored to No.17 buoy in Kethole Reach, almost opposite the town of Sheerness on the Isle of Sheppey, Kent. She had been moored there for some days – it is believed that the ship had to take on coal from the airship base at Kingsnorth on the Isle of Grain, brought to her by lighter. Many of her crew had been given leave the previous day. They had returned to their ship by 07.00 on the morning of 26th November and it was believed the full complement was onboard. The usual ship's routine was taking place. Many officers and men were having breakfast below, others were going about their normal duties. A band was practising while some men were engaged in drill. At 07.50 disaster struck (Plate 8).

A huge explosion ripped *Bulwark* apart. A roaring and rumbling sound was heard and a great sheet of flame and debris shot upwards. The ship lifted out of the water and fell back. There was a thick cloud of grey smoke and some further explosions. When the smoke eventually cleared the *Bulwark* had sunk without trace, but some time later a portion of the vessel could be seen about four feet above the surface of the water.

Out of the complement of 750, no officers and only 14 sailors survived, two of whom subsequently died of their injuries in hospital. Fred Travers was among those who lost their lives. His body was not recovered for burial.

The explosion was heard in Whitstable, 20 miles away, and in Southend where the pier was shaken by the explosion but not damaged. Ships anchored off Southend holding German civilian prisoners claimed they saw "a dense volume of greenish smoke which lasted for about ten minutes". The nearby areas of Sheerness and Rainham took the brunt of the blast with reports of damage to property being made. Rumour began to run wild amongst the residents. Some claimed it was the expected and feared Zeppelin raids commencing, others said that a periscope had been sighted and the *Bulwark* had been sunk by a submarine. Others thought that espionage had taken place and were on the look out for suspicious people in town. All these rumours were later discounted. Here are some of the witness descriptions:

From the battleship *HMS Implacable*, next in line at the mooring: "From the depths of a huge pillar of black cloud, flames appeared running down to sea level. There followed a thunderous roar, then a series of lesser detonations and finally one vast explosion that shook the *Implacable* from mastheads to keel".

From the battleship *HMS Formidable*: "When the dust and wreckage had finally settled a limp object could be seen hanging from a wireless aerial. When retrieved it was found to be the Engineer Commander's uniform jacket".

From the battleship *HMS Prince of Wales* (Fred Travers's previous ship): "Smoke issued from the stern of the ship prior to the explosion. The first explosion appeared to take place in an after magazine".

That afternoon, Thursday 26th November, Winston Churchill, the First Lord of the Admiralty, made the following statement to the House of Commons:

"I regret to say I have some bad news for the House. The *Bulwark* battleship, which was lying in Sheerness this morning, blew up at 7.35 o'clock. The Vice and Rear Admirals who were present, have reported their conviction that it was an internal magazine explosion which rent the ship asunder. There was apparently no upheaval in the water, and the ship had entirely disappeared when the smoke had cleared away. An inquiry will be held tomorrow which may possibly throw more light on the occurrence. The loss of the ship does not sensibly affect the military position, but I regret to say the loss of life is very severe. Only 12 men are saved. All the officers and the rest of the crew, who, I suppose, amounted to between 700 and 800, have perished. I think the House would wish me to express on their behalf the deep sorrow with which the House heard the news, and their sympathy with those who have lost their relatives and friends."

On 28th November, a naval Court of Enquiry (President, Rear-Admiral E.F.A. Gaunt) established that it had been the practice in *Bulwark* for ammunition for her 6-inch guns to be stored in cross-passageways connecting her total of 11 magazines. It was suggested that, contrary to regulations, 275 6-inch shells had been placed close together, most touching each other, and on the morning of the explosion some touching the walls of the magazine. It was further suggested (but of course there was no proof) that cordite charges stored alongside a boiler room bulkhead could have overheated; and that the fusing mechanism of one of the shells stored in the cross-passageways could have been weakened by damage, causing the shell to become 'live' (Plate 9). If it had been dropped point down, a chain reaction of explosions could have been set off among all the shells stored in the cross-passageways.

But at the Kent Coroner's inquest on 16th December into the tragic loss of the crew of the *Bulwark,* Rear-Admiral Gaunt stated that there was no evidence to suggest an external explosion and no evidence of treachery or of loose cordite. However loose cartridges had been found in the 'cross ammunition passages' but this had no relation to the cause of the explosion. A Commander Wilton confirmed that every cartridge onboard had been traced (by divers) and no evidence of loose cordite had been found. Although the jury were not fully satisfied with this explanation, a verdict of accidental death was returned.

Frederick Hubert Reginald Travers No 6012 Acting Leading Stoker (Plate 11) was awarded the Star, the Victory Medal and the British War Medal.

The accompanying picture of a battleship munitioning (Plate 10) gives an impression that the handling of ammunition in the early 20th century was somewhat haphazard and not an easy or pleasant evolution. *Bulwark* may not have been the only ship to have acted in contravention of ammunition regulations.

There were other ships to be lost by explosion in the First World War. These include:

HMS Queen Mary (with the loss of 1266 officers and men) at the Battle of Jutland 31st May 1916. Her magazines exploded shortly after she was hit twice by the German battle cruiser *SMS Derfflinger*. It was thought that unstable cordite may have been a cause but also that ammunition hoists were not protected from 'flash'.

HMS Indefatigable (with the loss of 1017 men) at the Battle of Jutland. Designed to take heavy hits without sinking, she was hit by two volleys from *SMS Von der Tann*, the first causing a low-order explosion in "X" magazine that blew out her bottom and the second hitting the forward magazine.

HMS Invincible (with the loss of 1026 men) at the Battle of Jutland. When 'Q' turret was penetrated by enemy gunfire the midships magazine exploded and that possibly ignited 'A' and 'X' magazines.

HMS Defence (with the loss of between 893 and 903 men) at the Battle of Jutland. Two German salvoes from *SMS Friedrich der Grosse* caused the 9.2-inch magazine to explode. Cordite charges caught fire in the ammunition passages to the adjacent 7.5-inch magazines which detonated in turn.

It is not clear whether *HMS Black Prince* (see Chapter 11) was lost (with 760 men) at the Battle of Jutland through the explosion of her magazines but it is possible.

The Germans lost 2551 men at Jutland, the British 6094 of whom

4969 were on board these five ships.

HMS Vanguard (with the loss of 804 men) at Scapa Flow on 9th July 1917. It is believed that an unnoticed stokehold fire heated cordite stored against a bulkhead adjacent to one of the two magazines which served the amidships gun turrets "P" and "Q". She sank almost immediately.

HMS Glatton (with the loss of 79 men). On 16th September 1918 the newly completed Monitor was in Dover Harbour. A low-order fire in the midships magazine ignited the cordite stored there. Flames spread aft. The Captain ordered both the forward and after magazines to be flooded. The forward magazine was flooded but when it was found impossible to flood the after magazine because the flames prevented access to the magazine flooding controls, the Senior Naval Officer Dover ordered the destroyer *Cossack* to torpedo and sink the ship. She fired two 18-inch torpedoes but the armour of *Glatton* was too strong so the destroyer *Myngs* with her 21-inch torpedoes was ordered to sink her. She capsized and the fire was doused. There was an ammunition ship berthed close by so if *Glatton* had exploded there could have been a really massive explosion affecting all of Dover.

There was, of course, a Court of Enquiry which established that the initial explosion had occurred in the midships 6-inch magazine situated between the boiler and engine rooms. The Court noted that a habit of the stokers was to pile the red-hot clinker and ashes from the boilers against the bulkhead directly adjoining the magazine to cool down before they were sent up the ash ejector. The magazine was considered to be well insulated with five inches of cork, covered by wood planking 0.75 inches thick. The Court asked that the magazine of *Glatton*'s sister ship *HMS Gorgon* should be emptied and examined. One finding was that some of her cork lagging was missing and rolled up newspapers inserted instead but nothing was conclusive except that slow combustion of the cork lagging could have led to the ignition of the cordite in it and that might have caused the explosion.

It seems clear that in every case there was ignition of cordite or a direct hit into one or more magazines. One is left with the impression, a hundred years later, that naval design and some habits of the era could and should have been better.

I mentioned that a Court Martial had taken place in *HMS Bulwark* in Portland harbour three weeks before her death and that it concerned decisions made during the pursuit of *SMS Göben* (a battle cruiser) and *SMS Breslau* (a light cruiser) in August 1914. This pursuit happened in the Mediterranean so Fred Travers was not in that theatre of naval events at the very beginning of hostilities with Germany. To put the pursuit into perspective it should be noted that *SMS Göben* was armed with ten 11-inch guns and had a top speed of 27 knots and *SMS Breslau* was fitted with twelve 4.13-inch guns and had a top speed of 27.5 knots.

The accused was Rear-Admiral Ernest Charles Thomas Troubridge; the charge against him being that "while commanding the Mediterranean Fleet's 1st Cruiser Squadron he failed to bring the German ships *SMS Göben* and *Breslau* to action" in the first days of the war. This Cruiser Squadron consisted of *HMS Defence* (his flagship) (four 9.2-inch guns, top speed 23 knots), *HMS Black Prince* (in which Petty Officer Albert Tiltman from Powerstock was serving) (six 9.2-inch guns, top speed 23 knots), *HMS Duke of Edinburgh* (six 9.2-inch guns, top speed 23 knots) and *HMS Warrior* (six 9.2-inch guns, top speed 23 knots).

His Commander-in-Chief, Mediterranean was Admiral Sir Archibald Berkeley Milne who, on 2nd August 1914, had sailed the Cruiser Squadron from Malta together with *HMS Indomitable* and *HMS Indefatigable*. These two ships were initially sent west towards Gibraltar to prevent the German ships escaping into the Atlantic. Other ships available to join the Cruiser Squadron were the light cruisers *HMS Chatham, HMS Gloucester* and *HMS Dublin*. The orders to the Commander-in-Chief and passed on to Troubridge were from Winston Churchill (First Lord of the Admiralty) and stated (*inter alia*) "In the early stages of the war, should we become engaged in it, avoid being brought to action against Superior Forces". Troubridge was also informed that *Göben* must be shadowed by two battle cruisers and the approaches to the Adriatic Coast must be watched by cruisers and destroyers to prevent a sortie by the Austrian fleet.

In compliance of these orders, Troubridge proceeded towards the approaches to the Adriatic. On 3rd August at 15.19 the C-in-C detached *Indomitable* and *Indefatigable* to search for the *Göben* and

Breslau, commanded by Admiral Souchon, west of Sicily. In fact the two battle cruisers located the Germans at 09.30 on 4th August but as Germany was not yet at war with Britain no violence ensued and *Göben* and *Breslau* proceeded east towards Messina. Milne had reported that he had contact and the position of that contact but he neglected to inform the Admiralty that the Germans were heading east. However the light cruiser *HMS Dublin* maintained contact until this was lost off the north coast of Sicily.

At 01.45 on 5th August, Troubridge received the Admiralty general signal that hostilities were to commence at once against Germany. At 16.00 on 5th August he was informed that *Göben* was in Messina. The German ships refuelled their coal bunkers there but although international law only allowed them to be in a neutral port (which at this stage it was) for 24 hours the Italians allowed them to stay for 36 hours. Meanwhile the Admiralty ordered Milne to respect Italian neutrality and stay outside the 6-mile limit from the Italian (Sicilian) coast. Despite the extra time, *Göben*'s fuel stocks were insufficient to get her to Constantinople (where higher command had ordered him to go) so Souchon had made a rendezvous with another collier in the Aegean Sea.

When the German ships departed Messina at 18.15 on 6th August they sailed through the southern exit to the Straits of Messina, covered by *HMS Gloucester,* heading for the Eastern Mediterranean. *Gloucester* reported that the Germans were heading north east for the Adriatic (east of Italy/west of Greece) in a feint which caused Troubridge to try to intercept them in the mouth of the Adriatic. *Gloucester* then reported them steering south east so Troubridge, realizing he had been hoodwinked, ordered two destroyers and the light cruiser *HMS Dublin* to launch a torpedo attack on the Germans. *Breslau*'s lookouts spotted the destroyers when *Gloucester* tried to engage her but in the darkness the Germans managed to evade their pursuers. At this stage Troubridge became convinced by his Flag Captain, Fawcett Wray, that it would be suicide for the squadron to carry on and fight the bigger and longer-ranging guns of the *Göben*. In tears, Troubridge ordered the chase to be abandoned; he signalled to his C-in-C at 04.49 on 7th August: "Being only able to meet *Göben* outside the range of our guns and inside his, I have abandoned the chase with my squadron. *Göben* evidently going to the Eastern Mediterranean".

With no further attempts being made to effect an engagement, not even in darkness (there was no Radar in those days), *Göben* and *Breslau* refilled their bunkers from a collier off the island of Donoussa near Naxos and proceeded up the Aegean (east of Greece). They entered the Dardanelles on the afternoon of 10th August. Turkey was at this time still a neutral country, bound by treaty to prevent German ships from passing through the Dardanelles Straits. To get round this difficulty, it was agreed that the two German ships should become part of the Ottoman navy and this happened on 16th August. On 23rd September Souchon was appointed commander-in-chief of the Turkish fleet.

Göben was renamed *Yavuz Sultan Selim* and *Breslau* was renamed *Midilli*; and their German crews donned Ottoman uniforms and fezzes! The consequences of the Royal Navy's failure to intercept *Göben* and *Breslau* were not immediately apparent but there was a feeling of humiliation such that Milne and Troubridge were censured. Milne was recalled from the Mediterranean but exonerated of any blame but Troubridge was subjected to a Court of Enquiry which led to his Court Martial aboard *HMS Bulwark.* In the event he was 'fully and honourably acquitted' on the grounds that his orders were conflicting and he had chosen to obey the one which said he should avoid being brought to action against 'Superior Forces'. Nevertheless the feeling was that this action was, as far as fleet morale went, a poor start to the anticipated demonstration of British command of the seas.

It is now considered that the gift by Germany of the two modern warships was to a great extent the 'trigger' for the Turks (up to now neutral) to enter the war on the side of Germany and the Central Powers. Denied delivery of two warships on order from British yards, the generosity of the Germans was, to Turkey, the clearest of indications which side she should support. This allowed the Central Powers to fight for two years longer than they would have been able to on their own. The war extended to the Middle East and had an effect on the course of the war in the Balkans. Had the war ended in 1916, some of the bloodiest engagements, such as the Battle of the Somme, would have been avoided. Also the United States might not have been drawn from its policy of isolation to intervene in a foreign war. Turkey, by allying itself with the Central Powers, had to share their fate in ultimate defeat, whereupon the victorious allies carved up the collapsed Ottoman Empire, creating many new nations including Palestine, Syria, Lebanon, Saudi Arabia and Iraq and starting the idea of a Jewish state in Israel for the first time. Also the closure of Russia's only ice-free trade route through the Dardanelles effectively strangled the Russian economy and was a critical contributor to the 'revolutionary situation' in Russia which would lead to the October Revolution.

Returning to the fortunes of the *Göben* and the *Breslau*, these now-Turkish ships proved to be big players in the Black Sea, fighting for Turkey against the Russians for the rest of the First World War and their many engagements with units of the Russian fleet make exciting reading for those interested in naval encounters. There were times when *Yavuz Sultan Selim* and *Midilli* were again in action against the Royal Navy, firstly on 25th April 1915 when *HMS Queen Elizabeth* and *HMS Lord Nelson* were in the region of Gallipoli but could not engage them, and between 20th and 24th January 1918 when *Yavuz, Göben*'s shortened title, and *Midilli* were in action with *HMS Lizard* and *HMS Tigress* at the Battle of Imbros. This battle resulted in the sinking of the Monitors *HMS Raglan* and *HMS M28*. *Midilli* struck several mines and sank; *Yavuz* hit three mines as well but managed to beach herself intentionally just outside the Dardanelles. The British tried to attack her with bombers from No.2 Wing of the Royal Naval Air Service (from *HMS Ark Royal*) but their bombs were not heavy enough to inflict serious damage. The Monitor *HMS M17* had a short attempt to shell *Yavuz* but had to withdraw to escape Turkish artillery fire. Then the submarine *HMS E14* was sent to destroy the damaged ship but was too late as *Yavuz* had been towed to the safety of Constantinople to be repaired. She remained in active service until 1950, being scrapped in 1973.

Richard Carpendale

Richard Carpendale is a former Naval Officer who specialised in Anti-Submarine Warfare and commanded the frigates *HMS Keppel*, *HMS Grenville* and *HMS Lowestoft*. He served in the Sultan of Oman's Navy in command of the Naval Base at Muscat from 1986-1989. He was the Administrator of the Romanian Orphanage Trust from 1990 to 1993 and a Citizens Advice Bureau adviser up to 2010. With his wife, he has kept a small flock of sheep since 1985.

CHAPTER 7

Fred Symes
Royal Garrison Artillery
Died Angle, South Wales 25th March 1915

By now, it will be well known that two thirds of the personal documents of First World War soldiers were destroyed in a Luftwaffe Second World War bombing raid. A key point to be made of the men of our Parish lost in the earlier war is that their family names survive within the local and broader communities. Prior to going on to full development, part of the Team's essential feasibility test of this subject had been to ascertain whether the information we needed might be found among identifiable relatives.

An arrangement was made with the *Bridport News* to allow each of the Project's researchers the use of the newspaper's two centre pages every week over a three month period. The disparity of knowledge between cases soon became apparent although, generally, the individual contributions strengthened over time. With only two exceptions, the researchers used their allotted two pages with much still remaining to be said. The exceptions were the submissions made on behalf of our man Fred Symes and Adrian Semmence's Sidney Styles. The *Bridport News* reassured their readers we had been enjoying our detective work! Nevertheless, so short were we of facts that Fred Symes' coverage shared one edition's centrefold with Sidney Styles. We came to the conclusion that if the information is truly unavailable, that is something which could not be circumvented. Adrian Semmence faced that reality and concentrated his study of Sidney Styles upon family connections. If however the information is out there somewhere, the lesson which arises from the consideration of this chapter is that you have to create your own luck. Our Community would expect nothing less.

Fred Symes was born in Loders on 25th March 1883 to Gaius and Mary Symes (née Warre-Symes). He was one of nine children, five of whom survived birth. Gaius was a farm labourer and lived in Loders. Various census returns show Gaius lived in the Loders area until he moved to Clifton, Bristol where he and Mary were married. Their first child, Gaius junior, was born there. The family moved back to Dorset and the 1881 census shows them living in Larkham Lane, West Milton. By now there were four children. Gaius junior, Robert, Fred and Walter. The census shows all the children except Gaius were born in Loders. Fred Symes grew up in this area and the 1901 census shows the family minus Gaius junior (who died aged 20) living in Nettlecombe. Robert, now 19 years old, is described as a labourer. Eighteen year old Fred is described as a 'Carter on Farm'. The youngest brother Walter, 15 years old, was a 'Thatcher's Assistant'.

It appears Fred earned his living as a labourer, presumably mainly on farms. He married Annie Mills Slade, who was born in Portland, in the third quarter of 1910. The 1911 census shows Fred had moved alone to South Wales and was lodging with William Henry Lloyd at 61 Pentwyn Avenue, Penrhiwceiber, Rhondda. He was working at this time as an underground collier, presumably as work was scarce in Dorset. At this time, Annie was living with her parents, John and Agnes Slade, at Chapel Cottage, West Milton. Annie bore a daughter who was named Eva S.S. Symes in the third quarter of 1911.

Fred returned to Dorset before enlisting in Dorchester. 17134 Gunner F. Symes joined 5th (T) Company the Royal Garrison Artillery (RGA). The RGA was one of the Royal Artillery's three branches. The other two were the Royal Field Artillery (RFA) and the Royal Horse Artillery (RHA). The RFA's equivalent to the Second World War's quintessential close support gun, the 25-pounder, was the 18-pounder. Sidney Styles had joined the RFA. The RHA was equipped with a 13-pounder but it soon became clear that the RHA had become obsolete in the new conflict environment to be found on the Western Front.

Fred's was a Training Company located at East Blockhouse near to Angle, Pembrokeshire. East Blockhouse, one of a pair allegedly designed by Albrecht Dürer for King Henry VIII, guarded the entrance to Milford Haven, one of the world's deepest natural harbours where the Allied Navy D-Day Strike Force assembled. The Henretian guntower at West Blockhouse on the opposite side of the haven was destroyed when the 19th century West Blockhouse defences were built. Today, the term East Blockhouse refers to the entire 16th-20th century complex which in Symes's time was a self-contained unit, a small elevated settlement with the sea to its front and a minefield to its rear. Searchlights had been set into the cliff face and an anti-submarine boom stretched between the Blockhouses. The gun emplacements are still there to be seen at East Blockhouse. The only original building remaining intact is the renovated home of the site owners, Jennie and Simon Robson. Elsewhere, there are flights of stone steps going nowhere.

Completed in 1903 at an estimated cost of £29,300, there were two 9.2-inch (anti-major ships) and two 6-inch guns (anti-destroyers/cruisers) representing the Battery during Fred's time there (Plate 12). The full complement of guns was never installed. The cost of

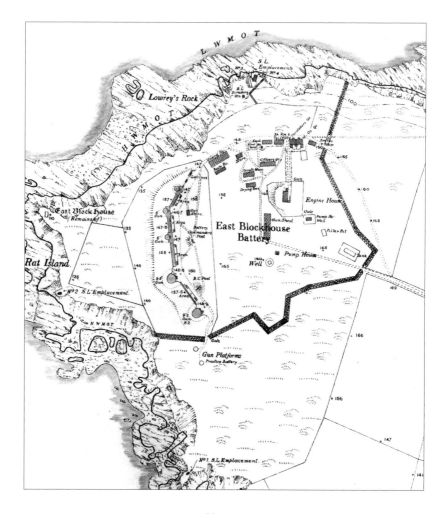

guns exceeded the building costs of the installation. East Blockhouse was the first of six lines of defence along the 8-mile length from the entrance of Milford Haven to Pembroke Dock. Given that guns took four minutes to reload, defence in depth was essential. Chapel Bay, half a mile to the west of Angle, built in 1891 and remodelled in 1901, is on the third line of defence. It is the home of George and Emma Geear, presently engaged in converting the site into a museum.

The mission was to protect the port and dock at Pembroke, part of the Western Coast Defences. The juxtaposition of heavy guns and fortifications represents the traditional concept of fortress-based artillery. The RGA's adoption of the Heavy and Siege Artillery roles on the Western Front, including train-mounted guns, embraced the requirement to apply plunging and flatter trajectory fire. Specialist RGA units included Anti-Aircraft Artillery, Mountain Batteries and the Royal Marine Artillery.

Fred had an operation in early 1915 before returning to East Blockhouse. It is possible that he did not enjoy the essential FE (Full Employability) category which would have made him eligible for posting worldwide. The limitation on his employment to UK-Base only would have meant he was barred from operational duties overseas, which was not the case for his elder brother Robert. Under normal circumstances it would have been thought Fred had the apparent prospect of serving out the war safely in a risk-free environment whereas brother Robert who fought in the trenches at Ypres had little prospect of enjoying a full life. These were not normal circumstances. Interestingly, the Army sent soldiers of above-average intelligence to RGA Fortress posts. Some had to be familiar with and adept at trigonometry.

Fred's was an interesting family. Records reveal both his father and uncle to have been committed to Dorchester gaol for poaching rabbits. The punishment appears not to have fitted the crime, yet it was a blessing that these indiscretions had not occurred earlier in their lives when the standard punishment was Transportation to Australia. New South Wales ceased taking UK prisoners in 1840, Tasmania in 1853. Close to Port Arthur, Tasmania's internment facility, there is a long pavement, each paving stone bearing the name of a former prisoner, details of his or her crime and the punishment awarded. Study of the paving stones reveals poaching to have been a qualifying crime yet what is shocking is the discovery of children's names included in the mix of slabs. Trivial offences such as stealing potatoes were deemed sufficiently serious to justify the separation of a child from his/her family. There was an element here of compassion, as seen in the very different treatment of hardcore criminals and those who had been the victims of harsh justice.

The all too evident threat of imprisonment was not the deterrent it might be thought to have been. Certainly, landowners actively sought the charging of miscreants *pour encourager les autres*. The truth of the matter is that labourers had a very limited, unsatisfactory diet. Poaching was a calculated risk. Those who took rabbits from the estates were providing a service to the owners for which, in return, and if not apprehended, they took away free food of a reasonable quality. Before the First World War, many estate workers were employed as game wardens. These workers could not claim theirs to be a reserved occupation. They joined the war, never to be re-employed in the quantity experienced before 1914.

The tools the poachers used for their business were the gin trap and the snare. The gin trap was a cumbersome, cruel metal device which was permitted by law to be in use until 1956 – in use by the landowner, that is. The poacher laid the device across a rabbit run, opened the spring-loaded jaws and hammered a metal stake into the ground. When the rabbit stepped on the plate between the jaws they snapped shut, securing or amputating the animal's leg. It was frequently the case that the sounds of an animal in pain and distress alerted either a game warden or a fox. The game warden bided his time until the poacher put in an appearance to check his traps, whereupon he would be arrested. The snare is an altogether easier device to handle, self-throttling and operated by the animal. The last licensed rabbit trapper on Castlemartin Artillery Range had 500 snares. In a good area he could catch up to 400 rabbits in a 24-hour period.

Fred Symes died on his 32nd birthday, 25th March 1915. Major Burnett of 57 Company RGA wrote to his widow Annie in West Milton:

"Dear Madam, I very much regret having to inform you that your husband, Gunner Fred Symes, was accidentally killed at East Blockhouse yesterday by falling over the cliff. I am sure the officers, NCOs and men of this company sympathise in this sad bereavement, and he will be missed by all in his battery, as he was a good comrade and a popular soldier."

The inquest was recorded in the daily register of deaths referred to the Coroner on 26th March with a brief verdict of "accident or misadventure". That was not the end of the matter.

For a token fee, Pembrokeshire County Council Archive Office offers a search facility of local newspapers. As a result of our enquiry and payment of the fee, the officers searched four weekly newspapers covering the two-week period after Fred Symes' death "but found no report of his death or the inquest that was held on 26th March". Luck plays a major part in this business.

We have a Central Control which monitors specialist genealogy sites. Most of the hits occur on first release. Since there is no budget, the modus operandi has been to sign-up for the short term but to withdraw when a new tranche of investment is sought by the operators. That was the case with www.forces-war-records.co.uk However, the operator's offer to rejoin for £5 appeared to be a good investment. It was more than that for, having saturated the site, there was one man in particular who identified himself as a veritable Welsh wizard in drawing information out of four newspapers now a hundred years old.

He referred back to us the quest of the relatives of Frederick George Biles of the 10th Hampshire Regiment who died at Gallipoli on 10th August 1915. The family's appeal for information appeared in the English *Western Gazette* dated Friday 19th November 1915 in an item titled 'Tidings Wanted of Soldiers Reported Missing'. Also found in 'Our Local Roll of Honour' – a list of those dead or wounded – in the *Western Gazette* dated Friday, February 5th, 1915 was a photograph on our wish list of George Galpin (Plate 7).

Of particular relevance to our case was an identical news item published in both *The Cambria Daily Leader* of Wednesday, April 7th 1915 and the *Mid-Glamorgan Herald and Neath Gazette* of Saturday, 10th April 1915:

"SOLDIER SLIPS OVER CLIFF. The tragic fate of a soldier at Angle on Thursday last was investigated by the County Coroner and a jury at East Block on Tuesday. The deceased was Frederick Symes of the 37th company (sic), Royal Garrison Artillery. It appeared that the deceased was engaged with others of his company digging a trench on top of the hill. Suddenly the ground gave way, and the deceased who had no chance of saving himself, was precipitated over the cliff and landed on the ground, sustaining severe injuries. A verdict of accidental death was returned".

The County Coroner had been misled. A subsequent military Board of Inquiry found that whilst on guard duty, Fred left his post to catch a rabbit. The cliffs there are known for their unsupported overhangs. It was also said that up on the edge of the cliffs, a rock gave way under Fred's feet and as a consequence he fell to his death (Plate 13).

Fred is buried in the Commonwealth War Graves plot behind the Church of St Mary, Angle, Pembrokeshire (Plate 14). There are ten official war graves from the First and Second World Wars, three headstones in slate, six in the traditional white Portland stone associated with Commonwealth War Graves on the Western Front and one of an irregular design. This latter headstone commemorates Jan Doucha, a Czech pilot of the Royal Air Force Volunteer Reserve. The Commission uses a variety of stones of differing colours and textures in its work around the world. Fred Symes' headstone is fashioned from slate. The white Portand stone has proven itself vulnerable to erosion which means a number of alternative stones have been sourced.

Fred had died when he should have survived the war. Nevertheless, he was recognised as having been among the war dead, was buried in a war grave and had his name put on the Parish war memorial. Whether one considers that to be right or not, it is not possible to look at this case retrospectively and second guess the Officers, the decision-makers, in-place at the time.

It was Fred's elder brother Robert who had been in great danger as he fought through the dispiriting months of 1914, culminating in the First Battle of Ypres. He was a member of the First Dorsets whose motto reflected the fact that they had been the First in India. The British soldier adopted a number of Hindi words into the English language, 'char' was one and 'Blighty' – a derivative from the Hindi word belayat – meaning the United Kingdom, another. Getting a 'Blighty one' referred to a wound requiring the soldier's casualty-evacuation home. Occasionally these qualifying wounds could be self-inflicted. A 'Blighty one' might also be an illness or disability and it was precisely one of these which saved Robert Symes. He contracted severe frostbite due to almost permanently having wet feet immersed in water frozen throughout an inhospitably cold winter of 1914. He was medically treated in Manchester before coming home and telling the *Bridport News* of his experiences.

"I was for seventeen days and nights in the trenches and the bullets were flying over our heads nearly all the time but very few of us were hit…we were holding a trench which our comrades had just taken and it was in a filthy state, just like standing in a mudpond. We stuck on as long as we could and then some of our men refused to stay there and the officers told us there was only one thing to do if we did not like it and that was to go over and take the trench the Germans were in. No sooner said than done…the Germans surrendered without firing a shot."

Robert Symes seemed remarkably cheery:

"Although I have been more than four months in the trenches, in sight of the Germans nearly all the time, if ever my country needs me was in another fix, I would volunteer again. I could stay here and tell you enough to fill a whole book".

* * * * *

So powerful were Pembrokeshire landowners that in their determination to achieve sobriety among their tenants, they often refused to have pubs on their land. Understandably, they held no sway over Angle's three pubs. They were not averse to bringing pressure to bear on more tolerant landowners. That was the case in 1915, the year Fred Symes died. The Speculation Inn is seven miles from East Blockhouse and three miles from Pembroke. Those who travelled out from Pembroke for Sunday Lunch and ale could make incontrovertible claims that their journey to this pub, sitting as it is just outside the three mile limit, was as a legitimate traveller.

In 1915, shortly after tenant Sarah Rodgers handed the pub over, the agent of the tolerant Orielton estate sent the new tenant a warning that his employer was coming under increasing pressure to close the pub. The squire refused to do this but did advise the incomer that he could make life easier for himself if he avoided three situations known to agitate the opposition:

- Allowing farm servants to leave horses waiting outside or to waste their time in working hours.
- Allowing young men to frequent the house in the evening.
- Allowing the house to be used directly or indirectly with rabbit catching or poaching.

The countryside was crawling with rabbits. There could be no argument that rabbit catching, for whatever purpose, was of benefit to crop growers. It also supplemented wages as an agricultural export, as can be testified by the stacked trays of prepared rabbit at Pembroke Station awaiting the express to rush the fresh meat to a hungry London. There was no rationing in 1915 yet there was also no obvious surplus of food. The Speculation Inn acted as a collecting point in the local area. Rabbits were exchanged for cash, not all of which found its way home. The collectors of the Castlemartin Rabbit Clearance Society and associates would then take the rabbits on to the Rabbit Factory in Pembroke for dressing. The soldiers at East Blockhouse enjoyed a potential monopoly of use of their War Department Land. Who is to disagree that a number did not capitalise on that freedom, either to catch rabbits for cash or supplement the traditional bully beef? The Speculation Inn still maintains its historic connection with the rabbit, as can be confirmed by reference to the menu:

Rabbit Pie
Devilled Rabbit
Rabbit Stew
Rabbit Curry

Tim and Megan Poole

Tim's family farmed King's Farm prior to his joining Dorset Police. His wife Megan is Welsh and works for the NFU.

CHAPTER 8

Sidney John Styles
Royal Field Artillery
Died Egypt, 12th August 1915

THE PROBLEM in accounting for Sidney Styles' contribution to the First World War is not so much the absence of personal records but rather that it would appear he made no definitive contribution. It would seem that the saying, 'they also serve who only stand and wait' applied to Sidney Styles. His Forces War Record reveals a young man from a large, working-class family living in southern England. His Birth Town is shown as Weymouth and his Resided Town is shown as Powerstock, Dorset. His Nationality is confirmed as British, his Date of Death as 12th August 1915 and his 'Fate', understandably, is simply expressed as 'Died'. Sidney was therefore an agricultural worker called up from a West Dorset rural estate to serve in the British Army and whose life ended on the eastern coast of the Mediterranean Sea, 2300 miles from home. I volunteered to research Sidney. My work takes me to Egypt. I was particularly interested to note that he was buried in one of the two large Commonwealth War Graves Cemeteries in Egypt.

Sidney Styles was born on 24th January 1894 at Franchise Court, Weymouth, to Emily Fanny Styles (née Keates) and her husband George Stickland Styles, a jobbing labourer. Sidney was their sixth child and his mother (who went totally deaf at the age of 24) would go on to have another two children. To continue Sidney's War Record, there is an anomaly here when we come to the next of kin information. He is shown as 'Brother of Miss F. Styles of 12 Rose Terrace, Westham, Weymouth' (Plate 15). Next of kin would normally be one of the parents. There is a hint of disharmony among the family. The family home was 12 Rose Terrace, renamed prior to the 1911 census as Granville Road (Plate 16). The house still stands there today, close to the Holy Trinity Church where Sidney was baptised and where many of the family events took place. Members of the Styles family still reside in Weymouth although none had any knowledge or information about Sidney.

Of his military details, his rank is shown as Gunner, his Service Number was 11695 and his location at the time of his death is shown to be Egypt. The revelation of his campaign medals, given that he had not taken part in any campaigns, is a surprise. He received posthumously Pip, Squeak and Wilfred, namely the 1915 Star, the British War Medal and the Victory Medal. His Service is declared to be the British Army, his Regiment the Royal Field Artillery and under 'Battalion' appears 'C' Battery 60th Brigade. This was a unit formed as part of the First New Army, K1, sometimes designated in Roman numerals – e.g. LX Brigade.

The family was in the process of establishing a military tradition. At the turn of the century, three of Sidney's elder brothers took the King's shilling. Levi was in the Royal Scots Greys stationed in York. William and George both enlisted in Dorchester in 1902, William to the Royal Artillery and George to the Dorsetshire Regiment. In 1903, George transferred to the Royal Artillery to serve with his brother. He left the Service after a three-year engagement. His brother William served until 1920.

William was Sidney's oldest brother, serving in France in the 16th Divisional Ammunition Column, Royal Field Artillery, from August 1914 to May 1915, and with the Guards Division, formed in France that August. When Sidney died, William's wife Sarah was already four months pregnant and when William left the UK again on 19th February 1916, his wife was within three days of giving birth to their fourth child – the day after the beginning of the Battle of Verdun. They named their newborn son Sidney Verdun Styles. The Battle of Verdun, 21st February – 18th December 1916, did not directly affect the British. It was a French vs German battle. French morale waned dangerously towards collapse until the French emerged victorious. They lost 542,000 men, the Germans, 434,000. As a measure to take pressure off Verdun, the British Army, supported by a lesser number of French, attacked the Germans in the First Battle of the Somme 24th June – 13th November 1916. This Operation and the need for Germany to milk off 15 German Divisions to the Eastern Front, saved Verdun and destroyed the complete structure of Germany's junior Non Commissioned Officers. Britain lost 420,000 on the Somme, the French 195,000 and the Germans 650,000.

Sidney followed his two brothers into the RFA. In February 1915, the three six-gun batteries of 60 Brigade RFA, under command of 11th (Northern) Division, were reorganised to become four four-gun batteries titled A, B, C and D. It was the Operational Planners' intention that 60 Brigade RFA would take part in the same Second Gallipoli Landing which would take the lives of Fred Biles and Fred Hansford. The brigade sailed for operations in the Mediterranean early in July 1915 but when the rest of the division moved on to Gallipoli in August 1915, 60 Brigade RFA remained in Egypt. It would seem that Sidney's life had been spared being put at grave risk through serendipity. The fact is that the flat trajectory of the 18-pounder close support gun, unlike the howitzer, is limited in rough terrain. They are vulnerable to interdiction organised from higher ground, to which the crest clearance capability of the howitzer affords both better protection and effect.

Sidney Styles died in Cairo on 12th August 1915 aged 21. The *Bridport News* of 16th September 1916 said he had died of appendicitis. Had he not been in a high demand environment for acute Medical Services support, he might have survived. He is not buried in the large Commonwealth War Graves Cemetery at Heliopolis but in the Port Said War Memorial Cemetery on the Mediterranean coast. Port Said was an important British Military Hospital centre during the war, receiving the Gallipoli wounded from May to November 1915.

With his large family living in Weymouth, there appears to be no obvious reason why Sidney should have been in Powerstock. However, an entry in the Powerstock parish magazine of September 1915 announced the death of Sidney Styles "of Mappercombe", the estate for which Nettlecombe served as the dormitory hamlet. It would seem that he was working on the estate at the time of his enlistment. Plotting his siblings' lives by way of the 1901 and 1911 censuses reveals a large, intricate family with interesting if not entirely happy lives.

The daughters did not fare well. Alice died when she was eight and Mabel was in service at the age of thirteen. Both she and Emily had sons at the age of 19 and when Mabel died at the age of 22, her son went back to her family rather than stay with his father. Emily's son was also sent back to the family home – perhaps because he had no birth father registered and was illegitimate.

Sibling	Born	1901 Census	Status	1911 Census	Status	
Emily Fanny	1880	Age 21	Away	Age 31	Away	
William Henry	1883	Age 18	Away	Age 28	Away	Enlisted in the Royal Artillery in 1902 age 19.
George	1885	Age 15	Enlisted in the Dorsetshire Regiment in March 1902 age 18. Transferred to Royal Artillery in 1903.	Age 25	At home	Telephone operator
Mabel Bessie	1888	Age 13	Away	Died in 1910 age 22		
Levi Jesse	1890	Age 11	At home	Age 21	Away	Private in the Royal Scots Greys
Sidney John	**1894**	**Age 7**	**At home**	**Age 17**	**At home**	**Fishmonger's errand boy**
Alice Kate	1897	Age 3	At home	Died in 1905 age 8		
Charles Herbert	1900	Age 1	At home	Age 11	At home	
Arthur	1899			Age 12		Emily's son
Herbert	1907			Age 4		Mabel's son. She had died 1 year earlier in 1910

Sidney John Styles' name is one of the eleven to appear on Powerstock's First World War Memorial. He is not alone in having his name appear on more than one war memorial. He is also commemorated on Weymouth's War Memorial. On that same memorial is the name of his nephew, killed in a later war, Sidney Verdun Styles. He was a Royal Marine and died on D-Day, 6th June 1944, manning one of the twelve Landing Craft of the 557 Flotilla taking troops of the French Canadian Regiment-de-la-Claudiers to Juno Beach, Normandy, maintaining the French connection to the last.

The final attempt in the *Dorset Echo* to raise a response from the public of the life of Sidney Styles having passed unproductively, all that remains is to close this short account of this enigmatic man. His name on the Weymouth War Memorial and in Powerstock

Church, along with 10 of his contemporaries, is the only remaining acknowledgement of his life. We are provided with an important reminder why we set out on this exercise – lest we forget.

Adrian Semmence
A resident of West Milton

CHAPTER 9

Frederick George Biles
10th Battalion The Hampshire Regiment
Died Gallipoli, 10th August 1915

IS THAT all that is left of you, just a few letters on the First World War Memorial in Powerstock church? Who were you? What was it all about?

Frederick George Biles. Everything about him seems abbreviated – from what we know about him, his length of active service (five days), the cause of death ('Died'), even the name of his regiment. He was born in Poorstock (sic) and baptised in the Parish of 'Poorstock cum West Milton' on 29th August 1880 by the Rev. R.S.M. Dowell. His parents were George (a thatcher and hurdle maker, born in Poorstock in 1856) and Marianne (or Mary Ann) born in Symondsbury in 1852. They married in 1880 and settled in Whetley and had three more sons: Herbert, born in 1886, who became a farm labourer; James, born in 1892, worked at thatching, as did Fred and their father; Oscar, born in 1897. Fred died in Gallipoli on 10th August 1915.

As *The Royal Hampshire Regimental History* (by C.T. Atkinson, 1952) put it, after having named the ten officers killed at the same time and place, 'other ranks killed and missing came to 155'. As a private in the British Army, Fred was definitely among the 'other ranks' and, given the conditions in which he died, probably among the 'great unwashed' as well. Details of his life could well be described by his rank. Had he been one of the Great and the Good, like Winston Churchill or Lord Kitchener, who both had more influence over his death than he ever had, we could read book after book about him. All he gets is this, and the gratitude and remembrance of our small community that cannot begin to imagine what he went through.

We know his name, rank, regimental number (10303), date and place of death and posthumous medals (British 'War and Victory' and the '1914/15 Star'). We know that in the 19th November issue of the *Western Gazette* it was acknowledged he was missing (Plate 17). His parents pleaded for more information. We can also read his name on the Helles Memorial Panel. (Cape Helles is at the tip of the Gallipoli Peninsular, in other words, the northern side of the entrance to the Dardanelles Strait). Because of that we know what happened to him: 'Died'. His body was never recovered.

We can imagine him as a small boy free-ranging among the fields and lanes of Whetley and Poorstock with local children, or helping his father with the thatching. I wonder how the headmaster reacted whenever he skipped school to scare birds from the crops or help with the harvest, like Nick Poole in our 1999 pageant? In 1914 he responded to the poster power of Kitchener's pointing finger: 'Your country needs YOU'. He wanted to help in the fight to keep us free and 'give us time'.

I wish I could have found out more about him. I got some help from the Royal Hampshire Regiment museum in Winchester, but they do not keep service records. The National Archives at Kew do, but Fred's were part of the 60 per cent of records destroyed by enemy action in 1940. The *Bridport News* at the time got little information from Poorstock about its men killed in action. There are about five 'Biles' with the phone code 01305 in our local directory. It would be good if this chapter rang a bell with someone who knows something.

Instead, Fred can be one of *our* Unknown Soldiers and serve his community again by representing 'Everyman', a symbol of the 720,000 British servicemen killed in action. By not being limited to and, possibly, distorted by the specific details of a particular individual, he can represent the universal.

One hundred years is a long time for us to imagine. Sixty years ago Winston Churchill was, once more, our Prime Minister, and L.P. Hartley wrote in his novel *The Go-Between*, 'The past is a foreign country'. Fred would find this country, now, very foreign, but perhaps not the countryside, at least not around here. What would he make of our school children now having mobile phones and being transported in cars the size of troop carriers? And what about our 'heroes' now, better paid, fed and trained than any of his pals, competing for cups and medals made of bronze, silver and gold. I think we need Fred to act as our 'go-between' and tell us about his 'foreign country'.

In September 1914 he answered Prime Minister Asquith's call for another 500,000 men to enlist. As many men joined up in a day as were normally recruited in a year. So successful was the recruiting that clothing and equipment ran out. The men's dignity and effectiveness were saved by good old 'makeshift and mend' until industry could gear up to meet the huge demand. Kitchener, who a month earlier had begun his campaign for volunteers for a New Army, insisted they had good accommodation and he raised their pay to three shillings (15p) a day.

Fred would have no doubt heard at the end of August of the British Expeditionary Force's defeat in the bloodbath of Mons in Belgium, and how the exhausted, terrified troops were protected and guided to safety by a vision of a shining angel. On the same day the Russian army was defeated on the Eastern Front. I wonder if Fred still shared the euphoria that had been so widespread when war was announced on the 4th of August and people believed that it would be over by Christmas, with Germany defeated? Kitchener knew better.

Fred joined the 10th (Service) Battalion of the Royal Hampshires in Winchester, part of the New Army, in September 1914. The men were moved to Dublin for training with the 10th (Irish) Division, and then moved to Mullingar. No, it was not all over by Christmas, although that was the Christmas Day where, in 'some corner of a foreign field' on the Western Front, British and German soldiers left their trenches, only yards apart, and chatted with each other in very bad French, exchanging goodies, like German cigars for English jam. No man's land was, in a brief moment of sanity, Everyman's land. The authorities were not amused. The men were not Playing the Game. The show had to go on – 100,000 casualties already, and counting.

In March 1915 these recruits were moved to the Curragh, 'training hard and their excellent behaviour and exemplary discipline made a profound impression' (according to Atkinson's *History*). Their next move was back to England in May 1915, for final preparations for The Front, involving training at Aldershot and the Ash ranges for 'intensive musketry and initiation into bombing'. Forty years later, when I was an Aldershot schoolboy, I used to gather old cartridges, enjoying the peace and quiet, blissfully unaware who had given them to me and at what cost.

An inspection by the King on May 28th and another by Kitchener a few days later gave the men an opportunity to show the remarkable progress they had made in well under a year's training. They were ready to go overseas, but where?

By now, the recruits would have been aware who the enemy was and where he was to be found. German submarines and mines were sinking our ships; their warships were shelling our east coast towns; a new threat, Zeppelin airships, were silently dropping bombs on British towns at night; another German first was the use of chlorine gas at Ypres. By the time the men were training in Aldershot, the Germans had torpedoed the *Lusitania*, killing 1400 civilians. No wonder people suspected of having German connections were being attacked in the streets and hundreds of suspected spies were kept in a 'concentration camp' in the Olympia complex in Kensington. Why, therefore, were Fred and the other recruits not being sent to fight on the Western Front?

By 1915 it was becoming clear that there would be stalemate on the Western Front, and Winston Churchill was desperately arguing for the opening of a radically different second front. The Dardanelles Straits were the only sea channel that our ally Russia could use to sail from the Black Sea into the Mediterranean or that we could use to supply them. The Russians were losing to the Germans on the Eastern Front because they kept running out of ammunition. If help could be supplied through the Straits the Russians might more successfully reduce pressure on the Western Front. The trouble was, the Straits were held by Germany's ally, Turkey. The other trouble was in the form of our dashing 40 years old First Lord of the Admiralty, Winston Churchill, and his imperial ambitions. He argued that if the Royal Navy could get through the Dardanelles' fortifications, Constantinople would just cave in, and Germany would be threatened from the rear. At a bold stroke the war could end and Britain would control the destinies of the near east.

The Royal Navy, though, had misgivings. Ships against entrenched forts were bad news. Ships against forts on both sides of a 100 miles long Strait, in places less than one mile wide, were very bad news. Committing ships at such a moment in the war to what was essentially a sideshow, far from the war's centre, was verging on the irresponsible. Admiral Fisher, our First Sea Lord, knew the Straits and their defences well. He was a good friend of Churchill and could not resist the latter's powerfully persuasive personality and enthusiasm. The French were in favour, so for the sake of the alliance, both countries sent battleships, albeit older ones.

Two other battleships had a role to play in this story. Britain had earlier considered it necessary for Turkey to acquire battleships of its own. Turkey was not involved in the build up to hostilities and she needed naval firepower to keep the strategically important Dardanelles open, so orders had been placed for two vessels with English shipyards, paid for by public donations in Turkey. By August 1914 one had been completed and the other soon would be. They had Turkish names and Turkish crews (already in England). Then, a day before the outbreak of war, on 3rd August, Churchill told the Turks he could not deliver. In the interests of national security the two ships would be needed for the Royal Navy.

The Germans were delighted to make good Turkey's loss at the expense of 'Perfidious Albion'. They sent the battle cruiser *Göben* and a cruiser, the *Breslau*, to the Mediterranean. The *Göben* could out-gun any Russian vessel and outdistance any British one. We had both in our gun sights on 3rd August, but the British ultimatum to Germany did not expire until midnight and the Cabinet had forbidden any act of war until then. Before midnight the two ships had slipped away and within days docked in the Bosphorus, with Turkish names and ownership and crewed by Germans disguised in Turkish fezzes. Germany now effectively controlled the Turkish navy and army and by the end of October 1914 the British, French and Russian governments delivered a 12-hour ultimatum to Turkey. The presence of the *Göben* effectively demonstrated Turkey's alliance with Germany against us, and the threat of its mere presence in hostile, mined waters added to the problems of the Allied naval campaign. A more potent German force multiplier proved to be Liman von Sanders who conducted a brilliant active defence fully supported by Mustapha Kemal.

In February 1915 the bombardment started well for us. Over 100 guns pounded away at long range, silencing all but one of the nearest earth forts. Panic was reported in Constantinople, all according to plan. Despite this apparent success, by March 18th the Anglo-French naval enterprise had failed to force the mine-strewn passage. We had lost the advantage of surprise by not keeping up the pressure. Instead the Turks had had time to lay more mines and install more guns. Despite the attack being led by the *Queen Elizabeth,* the largest warship ever to enter the Mediterranean, with her unprecedented fifteen-inch guns, we failed to break through the Narrows, the neck of the Dardanelles. Of the 176 guns defending the Dardanelles, only four had been put out of action; of the 392 mines (unfortunately undetected) not one had been cleared. The fleet lost 700 lives and three great ships. It retreated, never to return on a mission like this. The first landings at Gallipoli on 25th April proved inconclusive, leading to a three-month slog between the parties.

The naval withdrawal marked the end of an age: the Royal Navy was not omnipotent; imperial gunboat diplomacy could no longer be used to keep the indigenous people in line. The Turks fearfully awaited a renewal of the attack, but it never came. Winston Churchill wanted to try again, but was overruled. Fisher resigned – "Damn the Dardanelles! They will be our grave!"

This was when Fred Biles entered the war and the history of 'Poorstock'. By May 1915 he had completed his basic training in Hampshire. Meanwhile, while he was possibly wondering what it was all about and feeling a long way from home, army commanders on the spot in Gallipoli had made the case for reinforcing Gallipoli by three more British divisions. They decided to land an army on the peninsular forming the western part of the Dardanelles, from where they could open up an overland route to Constantinople.

The Gallipoli peninsular was an arid, apparently empty place of gullies and ravines, covered with scented scrub, which could be beautiful in summer but bitterly cold and eerie in winter. The planners had underestimated the difficulties of the rugged and virtually unknown terrain, particularly for this inexperienced 'New Army'. The only available maps were those produced for tourists.

On the 6th July 1915 Fred's battalion sailed from Liverpool in the severely overcrowded *Transylvania.* There was no space for the exercise needed to keep the men fit, and they had to be on constant lookout for enemy submarines, though they saw none. They were dropped on the island of Lemnos on the 26th July, among the hot dust and flies, suffering from thirst and diarrhoea. Incessant fatigues (personal and 'housekeeping' tasks) severely limited their training. They were, in other words, in poor shape, mentally and physically. Here they joined the Anzacs (Australian and New Zealand Army

Corps) who were also demoralized after being dug-in in cramped positions for so long. The French division had made a diversionary raid on the Asiatic side of the Strait before adding their weight to the main thrust.

On the afternoon of 5th August the 10th Hampshires embarked in small boats that served as ferries between the islands and the Gallipoli peninsular. They arrived under cover of darkness, wearing thin khaki drill and heavily laden with three days' rations and ammunition. They were packed so tightly in the little boats that movement was impossible (Plate 18). They were then transferred to lighters (flat-bottomed barges), from which they landed at daybreak on 6th August near the designated gully in which they

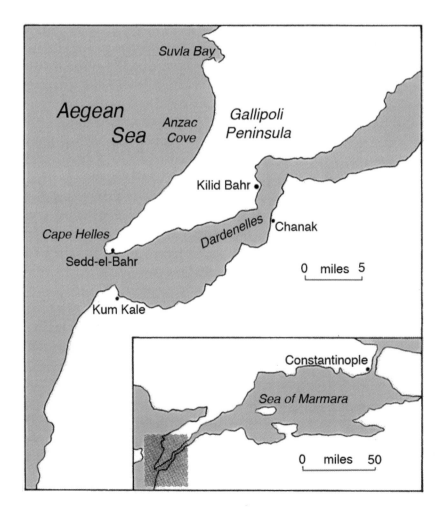

could hide in excavated shelters from Turkish observers and fire. It was important the Turks did not realise that five extra brigades were being concentrated there. After dark on the 6th August the forces advanced upwards and inwards, subsidiary attacks being made to distract the enemy's attention. This drew down heavy retaliatory shelling which cost the 10th Battalion a dozen wounded.

Early on 7th August they had to make a move up another gully. That proved futile, so they were sent back again to sit around and listen to flies buzzing, tummies rumbling and rumours flying. At 10 am on 8th August they filed off in another direction and waited until evening. Advancing again, they came under artillery fire, so had to advance across exposed ground in small parties and then struggle in single file along a narrow gully, choked with wounded making their way down. Progress was slow and tiring, keeping in touch was difficult, halts and delays were frequent and they had barely settled down in a bivouac area (temporary camp with limited cover) before, at about 10 pm, orders were received to push on. The guides then went wrong and led the column to the foot of a precipice. This meant turning round and retracing the route, doubly difficult in the dark and in the congested narrow space. The result of this was that by 5 am on 9th August Fred and the others were not in the right place to start the planned advance. By the time they were, at 6 am, the Turks were ready and well placed. The Hampshires waited until about 9 am and moved forward when reinforcements arrived (Plate 19). They were then stopped by heavy fire, machine guns and shrapnel, and could advance no further, so dug in, replicating the nature of war on the Western Front. No more counter-attacks were attempted during the night, but with daybreak on the 10th August the Turks came forward in great force. Such bungling was to become a hallmark of the whole campaign.

At this climactic moment, perhaps it is time to look at the Turkish perspective. Lieutenant Colonel Mustapha Kemal, their local commander, appears to have had something of Churchill's fearless impetuosity. He ordered six battalions to prepare for an attack at first light over the crest of a hill. He did not even know if the other side of the hill was precipitous, but decided the risk had to be taken. "I had come to the conclusion", he later wrote in his diary, "that we could defeat the enemy by means of a sudden, silent assault".

It was a desperate gamble. Our warships had the range of the hill 'to a yard' and during daylight hours it was impossible to rest on the crest of the hill: New Zealand machine-guns swept the slopes down which he proposed to attack. All the bitter experience of the campaign had proved over and over again that a frontal attack in daylight against machine-guns, artillery and entrenched troops was madness. If the attack failed, as so many of his attacks had failed in the past, there was nothing left: the British would have been able to capture the summit, occupy the whole of the adjacent ridge, dominate the towns en route to the Narrows, and from there – on to Constantinople! The campaign would have been over. Churchill would have been vindicated.

Kemal's senior officers begged him not to imperil everything in this reckless manner. He later commented: "As a matter of fact, they were right, but I was sure that success for us depended not only on the amount of men but also on their quality and using them to the best advantage. To wait would have given greater advantage to the enemy. Therefore, in spite of all their objections, I had to attack".

This is his description of the events of 10th August 1915: "It was nearly 4.30 am. After a few minutes it would become quite light and the enemy would be able to see our troops. Should the enemy infantry open fire with his machine-guns and should the land and naval guns open fire on our troops in our close packed formation I didn't doubt the impossibility of the attack. I ran forward at once and addressed the men: 'There is no doubt we shall defeat the enemy. Let me get in front first. When you see me wave my whip all of you rush forward together!'" (A bullet then smashed his wristwatch. He neither recorded this fact nor slowed down his pace towards the British trenches.)

The Turkish attack was an awesome spectacle. The astounded British gradually saw in the dim light dense masses of Turks advancing with fixed bayonets, not firing a shot. Trenches were overwhelmed almost at once, over 1000 of their British occupants killed within four hours. The New Zealand machine-guns roared into life and the warships sent shell after shell screaming into the Turkish troops, cutting them down, but they moved so quickly and were visible so briefly that large numbers of survivors reached the relative safety of the plateau. There, another British unit rose in desperation to meet them. Accurate details of what ensued have never come to light. By 10 am, with the sun high in the sky, the

British Commanding Officer and almost all his officers had been killed, and the remnants were falling back into the ravines, where many were lost and never heard of again. Even in the 1960s their bones were still being found.

*****

If we find it all confusing, knowing neither terrain nor strategy, we are not alone. A British Lieutenant Colonel arrived with a battalion on the previous day. He later reported: "No information as to the operations and plan of action was mentioned, nor what our side was trying to do". A lone horseman eventually arrived with orders to return to where they had just come from. When they got there, they were told to move somewhere else. The CO by now was wounded. This all took two days, during which the battalion never saw a Turk, suffered casualties from shrapnel and sniping, and exhausted itself in futile marching and counter-marching. A few days later a staff officer visited: "The officers in command of this part of the line were often unaware of the position of troops on their fronts and while I was there it was discovered that what for some days had been supposed to be Turks in Turkish trenches in the bushes on our left front were in reality our own men".

For another point of view different from that of an official history, which can be precise, factual and detached, but usually not too critical, we could look at Ronald Blythe's 1969 portrait of a Suffolk village, *Akenfield*, as portrayed by a few of its surviving inhabitants, interviewed by the author. For example, Leonard, born in 1896: "The first things we saw on Gallipoli were big wrecked Turkish guns, the second a big marquee. It didn't make me think of the military but of the village fêtes. Other people must have thought like this because I remember how we all rushed up to it, like boys getting into a circus, and then found it all laced up. We unlaced it and rushed in. It was full of corpses. Dead Englishmen, lines and lines of them, with their eyes wide open. We all stopped talking. I'd never seen a dead man before and here I was looking at two or three hundred of them. It was our first fear. Nobody had mentioned this. I was very shocked. I thought of Suffolk…" Fred Biles could well have been one of those corpses.

I wonder if he would have shared the sentiments of Rupert

Brooke in his elegiac poem *The Soldier,* prior to his embarkation for Gallipoli:

> If I should die, think only this of me,
> That there's some corner of a foreign field
> That is forever England...

Beautiful and moving, no doubt, but perhaps that could only have been written by someone who never quite made it there. Brooke died en route, of blood poisoning from a mosquito bite. Similarly, he would hardly have been so exultant about the prospect of action if he had realised how unprepared this most ambitious amphibious operation turned out to be – out of date intelligence; inaccurate maps; insufficient shells and mosquito nets; only two hospital ships; no dentists; DIY grenades (old tins); nobody knowing how many Turks were defending; appalling security...

The romantic, triumphant, pomp and glory of war needed a touch of realism, a glimpse of its obscenity. By the end, it got it. Wilfred Owen, killed in France in the last week of the conflict, left behind an unfinished poem called *An Imperial Elegy*:

> Not one corner of a foreign field
> But a span as wide as Europe...
> An appearance of a titan's grave,
> And the length thereof a thousand miles...
> And I heard a voice crying,
> This is the Path of Glory.

Finally, a word about those towering figures who had so much influence over the last few months of Fred's life:

Lord Kitchener visited Gallipoli in late 1915 and recommended withdrawal. He could not get on with politicians and his stature declined as the war dragged on, but he remained a hero to the public. On a mission to Russia in June 1916 his cruiser hit a mine. There were no survivors. The cruiser was the *Hampshire*.

Winston Churchill was sacked from the Admiralty in May 1915. He had quarrelled with his old friend Lord Fisher and was bitter about the guidance he had received from the admirals before the naval attack on the Dardanelles. In November 1915 he was dropped from the war cabinet. He admitted there had been 'personality problems', but denied impetuosity.

Mustapha Kemal was promoted to General during the War. Having helped push the British and the Allies out of Gallipoli, he then did the same to the Greeks out of Anatolia. When Turkey was declared a secular republic in 1923 he became President until his death, at 57, in 1938, having changed his name to Kemal Ataturk, 'Father of the Turks'. In the face of fierce internal opposition, he suppressed what he considered to be benighted Islamic traditions and introduced greater political, economic and educational opportunities, especially for women. For the rest of his life he dedicated himself to attempting to transform his country into a modern, democratic nation state.

As for Fred Biles, "the very hairs of your head are all numbered. Fear ye not therefore, ye are of more value than many sparrows. Are not five sparrows sold for two farthings (0.1p) and not one of them is forgotten before God?"

Roger Britton

School teacher, Surrey. Retired 1996, moved to Dorset. Ran a B&B until 2011. Currently doing a Foundation Art, Design and Media Foundation Diploma at Weymouth College.

CHAPTER 10

Herbert Frederick (Fred) Hansford
Queen's Own Dorset Yeomanry
Died Scimitar Hill, Gallipoli, 21st August 1915

HERBERT FREDERICK (Fred) Hansford was born in Nettlecombe 1878. His father and grandfather were butchers by trade. He himself would grow up to assist in the family business in Powerstock and still be there, unmarried aged 33, according to the 1911 census. However, his death would take place just over 1500 miles away on the Gallipoli peninsular fighting the Ottoman Empire.

Fred's parents – the impressively sounding father Frederick Russell Hine Hansford and mother Elizabeth Eloise Isabel Hine were married in Powerstock on 25th December 1877. Frederick was 23 and from Powerstock, and his wife Elizabeth from Nettlecombe. Herbert (Fred) Hansford was born sometime in 1878 (no precise date has been found yet). Very little trace of his childhood can be found other than mentions in the census returns and an entry in the school register that Fred Hansford pupil no. 486 was admitted to Powerstock School in January 1882. Mr Willett had been the school's headmaster for 34 years until his sudden death in September 1883. His successor was no spare-the-rod advocate, particularly when he found the school so disorderly. He 'administered corporal punishment to Fred Hansford for fighting and tyranny towards a younger boy. This boy, Hansford is the worst in the school. His language is filthy and his behaviour indecent. He corrupts all the other boys and is the terror of the girls'.

Although still a bachelor in 1911 and working in the family butchers, he did eventually marry sometime in autumn 1914, at Wantage, Berkshire. Fred was undoubtedly already serving in the (Queen's Own) Dorset Yeomanry at this time, as the Regiment was training with the other Yeomanry Regiments of the Berks and Bucks in Berkshire as part of the South Midland Mounted Brigade. However, his bride to be was not native to the South Midlands but rather someone who lived 'over the hill' back home in Powerstock.

Fred's wife was a young girl of 18, half his age, called Susan Mabel Osborne. She was born on 12th June 1896 in Crewkerne, into a farming family. In 1901, the census records that her father Benjamin Osborne kept a farm in Rampisham, but by the 1911 census they had moved off the Downs onto a farm in Melplash, where the then 14 year old Susan is listed as a 'farmer's daughter' doing 'dairy work'. Given Hansford's family butchery business it is conceivable that Fred could well have already met the young Susan Osborne, before leaving for the war with the Dorset Yeomanry, through his trade.

The Queen's Own Dorset Yeomanry (QODY) were one of many County based mounted territorial troops.

According to an historian of the Regiment, Charles Thompson, writing in 1921: "Throughout the mobilisation of the period the response of the yeomen of Dorset was admirable: and ex-yeomen begged to be re-enlisted, but owing to strict order on the subject, these could be only taken in limited numbers."

Given that Fred Hansford was already a relatively older soldier of 36 at the outbreak of war in August 1914, it could well be that he was already a long established territorial, indeed this could also help to explain his rank of Sergeant and very low regimental number, 8. The Dorset Yeomanry were formally assembled on the 5th of August. Sergeant H.F. Hansford is listed as being in No. 4 Troop serving under Lieutenant (later Captain) Alfred Douglas Pass (Plate 21). Therefore it is highly likely that Fred was one of those soldiers under Lieutenant Pass who marched through Bridport on the 10th August 1914. Initially the Dorset Yeomanry were stationed in different coastal areas, some even at West Bay, but by mid-September 1914 the whole Regiment was brought together at Sherborne.

At Sherborne the Officers were stationed at Digby Hall, whilst the other ranks were accommodated in the school buildings of Sherborne School. Here Thompson reports that: '… continuous training and inspections were the order of the day, but no ammunition was available to put the men through a musketry course, all being required at the Front in France'.

The regimental order books outline a routine of:

    Morning stables   6 am

Breakfast	8 am
Parades	9.30 am
Dinner	1 pm
Parades	2.30 pm
Tea	5 pm
Lights out	10 pm

Every man was expected to be in his billet by 10 pm.

However, 'Notices' for the 13th August show that conditions were not harsh as 'by kind permission the swimming bath at the King School will be open for troops from 5-6 pm daily'.

The first months of the war for the Dorset Yeomanry were relatively 'quiet'. After the majority of the territorials had volunteered to serve overseas, they were ironically sent to Berkshire to become part of the aforementioned South Midland Mounted Brigade. Throughout the autumn of 1914 they trained with the Berks and Bucks Yeomanry Regiments. Then, in the winter of 1914-1915, they were stationed in Norfolk against the threat of invasion, following the German seaborne bombardments of the East coastal towns of Whitby, Scarborough and Hartlepool. However this was to change in the spring of 1915, when the Dorset Yeomanry received its orders to go overseas finally to Egypt.

On the 7th April 1915 Fred Hansford, along with the 26 Officers, 506 ranks and 498 Horses set sail for Egypt on the two His Majesty's Transport ships, *Karoa* and *Commodore*. Despite the reportedly 'uneventful' journey, 30 horses were lost at sea. While simply stated, this recalls the many 'horrors' of the war experienced by animals as well as men, as shown graphically in Michael Morpurgo's story, 'War Horse'. Fred and his fellow soldiers arrived at 7.30 pm on the 21st April at El Zarieh which is north of Alexandria:

> '...where they pitched camp on a somewhat cold site, rendered less pleasant by a downpour of rain, much to the astonishment of the yeomen, who thought they were arriving in a rainless country.'

In Egypt, the Dorset Yeomanry continued their training but on the 22nd July they received official warning to prepare for service as dismounted troops. Wherever the Yeomanry were going, the much prized horses would remain in Egypt. Finally on the 14th August at 6.30 pm they embarked on ships again, this time for the Gallipoli peninsular and 'action' against the Turks of the Ottoman Empire.

As First Sea Lord, Winston Churchill had conceived of the idea of capturing the Dardanelles Straits and with it the route to Constantinople, thereby 'knocking out' one of Germany's key allies – the Ottoman Empire. It will be recalled that in March 1915, a Naval attack to 'rush' the Straits had failed following the sinking of several British and French ships. Then in April 1915, the Army was called to invade and capture the Gallipoli peninsular in order to support the Navy through the Dardanelles. However, the initial successful landings had not been followed through and a Western Front style system of trenches had been established, with its inevitable 'stalemate' as the machine gun proved too good a defensive weapon. The British general commanding the Army, Sir Ian Hamilton, had tried further landings up the Gallipoli peninsular involving famously the Australian and New Zealand Army Corps (ANZACs). By August 1915, one last attack to break through the Turkish lines was being planned. It was this offensive the Dorset Yeomanry including Fred Hansford would take part in.

Following the stalemate on the Helles front to the south of the peninsular and especially the failure to capture the strategically important town of Krithia, Hamilton had conceived of landing troops further north at Suvla Bay to try to take the important Sari Bair Range and other crucial higher ground. The landings at Suvla Bay began on the night of 6th August against light opposition but, as was so frequently seen throughout the campaign, the British commander, Lieutenant General Frederick Stopford, failed to seize the initial advantage he had of surprise and advance inland as much as he could. Little more than a beach area and the cliffs behind had been secured at Suvla. Quickly the Ottomans were able to strengthen their positions in the Anafarta Hills which would, to the Suvla Bay front, become yet another stalemate. Despite Stopford receiving reinforcements through further landings on the 7th and 8th August, an attempt to break through across the Anafarta Plain had failed by the 12th August, including the loss of the noted 'Sandringham Company' of men from King George V's Sandringham estate from the Royal Norfolk Regiment. Following this setback, Hamilton's staff then considered whether to evacuate both the Suvla and Anzac Bay areas. However, it was decided to make one last attempt to revive this campaign with an attack on the 21st August. It would be this offensive that Fred and his comrades would take part in.

Lieutenant Colonel Troyte Bullock (Plate 22) commanding the Dorset Yeomanry, writing in the front-line trenches a week after the attack on Scimitar Hill recalled what had happened in a letter to Lieut. Col. Colfox in England:

We left our comfortable quarters in Egypt Friday August 13th and evacuated to Alexandria that night, embarking the next morning on a very overcrowded transport put to sea that evening 14th reached our base on the peninsular on the mooring on the Wednesday 18th disembarking via launches and barges under shell fire. Luckily none of our brigade were hit, but one boat had a very narrow squeak. Rested in camp all thru the day Thursday 18th. On Friday 19th as night fell the brigade fell in and advanced to a place on the seashore 56 (m). I rested that night on a very narrow piece of beach under cover of the cliffs packed together like herrings. The only consolation was that some got to bathe in the sea. That afternoon (Sat 21st) we paraded with the rest of the Division about 3 pm and marched across 2 miles of flat salt marsh in attack formation to a hill crossing the open ground. The enemy opened up on us with heavy shrapnel fire and the division lost several officers and 60 men. On reaching the cover of the hill and calling the roll, seven men only of the Dorsets were reported wounded so the Regiment was most fortunate. At 4.30 pm an order came for the Brigade to advance and attack another hill about two miles distant, the infantry brigade to be on our Right to join in the attack on the Turkish trenches on the hill. We moved off 1st Berks Yeo, 2nd Dorsets 3rd line Bucks Yeo. through the scrub, some burnt and some burning from the effects of shell fire on the hill from our guns and over undulating ground.

We crossed our advanced trenches held by SW Borderers and Inniskilling Fusiliers, who had already made an attack, got on to the hill but had been driven out by shell fire. They were a good deal shaken and knocked about. The Turks kept up a heavy fire probably long ranged, indirect, and the bullets seemed raining on us. We did not get many casualties until the edge of the plateau forming the top of the hill was reached. Then we halted under cover of banks and partial cover thrown up by the infantry attack and reorganised for the attack. Some infantry (about 20-30) under a captain joined us and our Brigade ordered the push line now composed of Dorset,

Bucks and Berks, to attack.

Directly the push began, a hellish fire from machine guns and rifles opened from the trenches but some of the attackers got in. However in charging the trenches they had bombers and machine guns placed in the angles and they could not maintain themselves.

The brigade on our right never got within a mile of the hill to support us, so the attack failed and we all breeched on the edge of the plateau and awaited reinforcements provided by the infantry. I collected stragglers from the brigade accounting to some 50 men and held to 3.30 am. Some infantry then appeared and took over the line. Colonel Grenfell of the Berks having sent word that he had retreated to the line of infantry trenches previously crossed in the attack. I marched the remainder back there and under the cover of the hills from where the 2nd attack had started, where I found a field general dressing station.

Our casualties were very large.

The casualties were indeed very large - seven officers and 119 men had been lost. What exactly happened to Sergeant H.F. (Fred) Hansford is not known. However, the officer commanding his troop, Douglas Pass, was wounded and captured by the Turks[1]. Later on, after the war, Troyte Bullock recalled that during the action on the 21st August:

We reached our advanced trench, a very deep one which gave such good cover that there was a slight delay in getting over it. 'A' Squadron was leading, and this was the last I saw of Douglas Pass for some years, as he was hit soon after and taken prisoner.

One can perhaps surmise that Fred Hansford may well have been one of those who was killed following Douglas Pass going over the top.

The officer commanding the 2nd Mounted Division, (including the Dorset Yeomanry), Major General Peyton, whilst resting at Mudros, Lemnos some three months after the battle of Scimitar Hill, wrote to Colonel Colfox back in England reporting the efforts of the Yeomanry:

Their gallant Colonel Troyte Bullock led them into this action and he alone of all his officers came out unscathed, never was a desperate attack more gallantly led, never was the call of a Commander more bravely answered than by the men of the Dorset Yeomanry when Colonel Troyte Bullock acting under superior orders assaulted and captured the enemy's first line trenches. Many gallant men fell, perhaps the best known Nigel Learmouth, Sir Thomas Lees and Gray, but all were equally grand and the County of Dorset must have been stirred to its depths to read of their sons' bearing in the hour of trial.

Another officer of the Dorset Yeomanry, Major E.W.F. Castleman, would write of the action later whilst convalescing in September 1915, describing the bravery of men such as Fred but also the ultimate waste of their efforts.

The battle of the 21st was a fine performance for our men. We went in 280 strong and came out 140 and the terrible part was that the result was 'nil' – not from our own fault, but because (1) we started too late and darkness came on just as we took hill 70 and (2) the same old mistake was made by the chief powers – insufficient support to consolidate and make good the success.

The men were splendid - I never saw one of them show the slightest fear or hesitation to advance then, when the order was given, they were terribly handicapped by the loss of officers and their first baptism of fire was one of the most severe battles ever known to history.

Fred's death along with many in his and other units and regiments had resulted in very little if any strategic success. There would be no further Allied offensives on the Gallipoli peninsular. The situation in the Eastern Mediterranean became more complicated for the Allied forces with the entry of Bulgaria on the side of the Germans and Ottomans, as it meant a land route to supply the Turks would be established, including heavy artillery to pound British, Australian and New Zealand troops dug-in on Gallipoli.

Meanwhile conditions in the trenches were becoming unbearable for both sides. Dysentery and disease had already led to a great many casualties on both sides throughout the summer months. Then, as the winter of 1915 approached, a heavy rainstorm struck on 26th November, lasted three days and was followed by a blizzard at Suvla Bay. Troops found their trenches flooded, soldiers drowned and the flood washed the dead into their lines. The subsequent snow and cold temperatures then killed further numbers through exposure.

Following the replacement of Sir Ian Hamilton by Lieutenant General Sir Charles Munro as Commander in Chief for Forces in Gallipoli, the decision to evacuate the peninsular was taken. This led to Sir Winston Churchill unkindly remarking about Munro that, 'He came, he saw, he capitulated'. However, the evacuation was by all accounts the most successful part of the campaign, as not a single soldier was lost, despite some predictions that it could cost up to 30,000 men. Through the use of ingenious deceptions, such as a 'self-firing' rifle, (which was rigged in such a way that water dripping into a pan would lead to the trigger being pulled), troops had been withdrawn gradually. Suvla and Anzac Bay were evacuated on 20th December 1915 and the garrison at Helles was withdrawn on 28th December. The last British troops left the peninsular on 8th January 1916.

What was left of the Dorset Yeomanry stayed in Gallipoli until they were evacuated in October 1915, and the machine gun sections stayed right until the successful evacuation in January 1916. According to Charles Thompson, in his history of the Yeomanry, after nine weeks of fighting, of the 1800 men who had served with 2nd Mounted Brigade (Bucks, Berks and Dorset Yeomanry) 1000 had been casualties. Of the 200 men left, at the time of the withdrawal, (from the three regiments) only 65 Dorsets remained.

Those members of the Regiment who had stayed in Egypt with their horses, together with the survivors from Gallipoli, went on to take part in the campaign in Palestine against the Turks, and even took part in the famous cavalry charge at the Battle of Agagia in February 1916.

The Dardanelles campaign had been a disaster. Almost nothing had been achieved, the Straits had not been opened, Constantinople had not been taken and Turkey remained very much in the war, now bolstered with an important victory against the Allies. In total, the British and their Allies had over 56,000 dead and 124,000 wounded. Sergeant H.F. Hansford was just one of the 34,072 British dead.

His very young widow, Susan Mabel Hansford, went on to remarry a Thomas Charles Marsh in Bradpole Church on 31st December 1919. She lived until 1982 and died in Cheltenham, Gloucestershire at the age of 86. Fred Hansford's name went onto panel 17 or 18 on the Cape Helles memorial in Turkey for soldiers missing presumed dead from the Gallipoli campaign who have no known grave. The memorial designed by John James Burnet was unveiled in 1924. Fred's name also went onto the memorial in Powerstock Church and one in Powerstock School.

Major General W.E. Peyton who commanded the 2nd Mounted Division was to write of the Dorset Yeomanry:

> For Dorsetshire, August 21st 1915 and February 26th 1916 should be anniversaries to remember in connection with their County Yeomanry. A more gallant and splendid lot of officers and men I can never hope to have under my command.

In the course of my research and writing this chapter, I have come to realise that the History and Commemoration of the First World War is much more than the 'big sweep' of battles, generals and major geo-political changes but the history which is hidden behind every single name on the war memorials in every town and hamlet, in Great Britain, France and indeed in places all over the world. However, above all I hope I've done my bit to preserve the memory of Fred Hansford, from Powerstock, one of those 'gallant' men from Dorset.

Jean-Paul Draper
Head Teacher Powerstock School

[1] The original Prisoner of War (POW) card of Douglas Pass is on display and can be seen at the Keep Military Museum in Dorchester.

Sources:

Glyn, RH (1939) *A Short account of the Queen's Own Dorset Yeomanry 1794-1939*, Henry Ling, Dorchester

Thompson C (1921) *Records of the Dorset Yeomanry 1914-1916*, F Bennett & Co, Gillingham.

Papers relating to the Dorset Queens Own Yeomanry, (1915-1919), Ref D-DOY/A/6/5, Dorset History Centre. This resource includes letters from various officers recounting campaigns.

Dorset Yeomanry Part II orders 1915 with casualty list 1915-1916 (1915-16), Ref D-DOY/A/2/1/1, Dorset History Centre.

CHAPTER 11

Albert Tiltman
HMS Black Prince
Died Jutland, 31st May 1916

1878, THE YEAR in which Albert Tiltman was born, marked a watershed in European history. The Congress of Berlin, which opened in the hot summer of 1878, was convened to try and resolve the so-called Balkan Question, ignited once again by the Russo-Turkish War of 1877-78. It was chaired by the German Chancellor, Otto von Bismarck; Benjamin Disraeli, Britain's Prime Minister, recently enobled as Lord Beaconsfield, struggled from his sick bed in London, took the trains and ferry to Berlin, and became the other major figure in the heated negotiations which went on for a whole month.

There were many participating nations, each with their own agenda, but the decisions to award the former Turkish Slav province of Bosnia-Hercegovina to Austria Hungary, and the island of Cyprus to Britain are the two which affect our story. Hitherto, the recently united Germany had been recognised for its all-conquering Prussian army; by holding the Congress in Berlin, Bismarck established the 'new' Germany as a major diplomatic player.

Austria's prize spurred on the activists who wanted a united free Slav nation, centred on a Serbia which was given autonomy in the negotiations. A long fuse was lit, exploding when terrorists murdered the Archduke Franz Ferdinand, heir to the Habsburg throne, in Sarajevo in June 1914. Despite many efforts to limit any war to the Balkans, the Great European War broke out in stages in August of that year.

Turkey, the Suez Canal and the Great War will play a huge part in the future life of Albert Tiltman, born in the October of that momentous 1878. The bad fairy of coincidence, as we shall see, had started to spin her tangled web.

Albert was born on 26th October 1878 in East Street, Bridport.

His father, John William Tiltman, then aged 25, was employed as a carter at a brewery in the town. Albert's mother, named Eliza, was a year younger than her husband. Also living with them was Eliza's mother, Eliza Lacey, a widow aged 63, and Albert's two elder sisters – another Eliza then aged 4, and 3 year old Bessie.

Albert was baptized on 3rd August 1879 and a few years later probably went to school at St Mary's, then in Gundry Lane in the centre of the town. By the time of the 1891 census, four more boys and one girl had been born to the Tiltman family, and Bessie, aged 14, was shown as a general service domestic. Mother-in-law Eliza was still going strong at 79, but also living with them were two nephews, Frederick, 28, and another Albert, 22. Nephew Albert was a seaman in the Royal Navy and undoubtedly gave 'our' Albert the encouragement to follow in his footsteps. The house in East Street, where the family still lived in 1911, was shown in the census of that year as having only four rooms, 'including kitchen, but not scullery, landing, lobby, closet, or bathroom'. In 1891, 15 people lived there, and after that two more boys and one girl were to be born!

When Albert was born, Mr W.H. Smith, the newsagent immortalised by Gilbert and Sullivan, was First Lord of the Admiralty, and hence 'the ruler of the Queen's Navee'. The Navy, unstretched by any major conflict since the Napoleonic Wars, needed rousing from its somewhat torpid state. Steam had established its place instead of sail, and new warships were being built of iron and soon of steel. In Albert's time, there were to be major advances – turbines, oil fuel, big guns, mines, submarines, and torpedoes in which he was to specialise. Fortunately for the nation, the Navy found leaders like Scott and Fisher to drive ahead the necessary modernisation of warship design and manpower training in the face of strong opposition from the traditionalists.

So let us follow Albert's 22-year career in the Navy during this time of huge change, covering 20 years of peace and preparation, and ending in two eventful years of war against Germany.

Albert joined the Navy as a Boy Seaman, Second Class, on 17th January 1894, three months after his 15th birthday. This was nothing unusual as the Navy had employed boys on warships for many years – they were the powder monkeys of Nelson's day. He was 5 feet 2 inches tall, with fair hair and grey eyes, and was allocated an official number 177591 – Portsmouth – his base port. After enlistment he was sent down to Devonport to join *HMS Impregnable*, the training ship for boy entrants, moored in the lower reaches of the Hamoaze off Cremyll. *Impregnable* had been built at Pembroke Dock in 1860 as *HMS Howe*, changing her name when she replaced an older *Impregnable* as training ship in 1892. She had a wooden hull, was propelled by screw or sail, and was armed with 110 guns and looked like a ship of the line of 100 years before. Built at the same time as the first iron warship *HMS Warrior,* she soon became outdated and was placed in reserve up the Tamar until 1892.

An article in the *Grey River Argus* of November 1896 tells us what training the boys had to undergo. They first had to 'learn to use a needle, to be methodical, and to stow their clothes and other belongings in a large capacious bag which serves as a portmanteau'. They were taught 'bends and hitches, the management of sails, knotting and splicing, and the making of mats such as are used after a collision to reduce the inrush of water through a hole in the ship's side'. There were 12 classes spread around five decks, each under an instructor, learning about such things as yards and sails, anchors, morse and semaphore, and following a compass to steer a ship. The author also tells us that they had to learn how to swim (presumably over the side of the ship in slack water) and goes on to say that 'this does not always overcome their landlubberly dislike of more water than can be conveniently contained in a wash-hand basin'. Life was hard and primitive, the food probably very basic, and the ship very cold and damp.

Albert was soon transferred to *HMS Lion,* a smaller former second rate ship, which was moored by *Impregnable* and part of the same training establishment. There he completed his first year under training, passed his exams, was rated Boy First Class, and sent for further training to *HMS Boscawen.*

He served in her from February to May 1895. *Boscawen* had originally been *HMS Trafalgar*, a 120-gun first rate ship of the line, launched, coincidentally by Lady Bridport, at Woolwich in 1841. Queen Victoria and Prince Albert attended the launch with due ceremony and celebration. She was fitted with screw propulsion in 1859, and came to Portland to act as a training ship in 1873, replacing the original *Boscawen.* Portland Harbour was at that time protected by only the two south-most breakwaters, and rough weather often prevented the crew getting ashore. The Boys were paid little money

– in 1872 they received only 3 pence per week. Corporal punishment was frequent, and the ship was often in quarantine with outbreaks of scarlet fever. Albert was however nearer to home, and perhaps he travelled to see his family by train from Portland via Weymouth, Dorchester, and Maiden Newton, and finally to Bridport. (*Boscawen* is today the name of the local Sea Cadet unit, thus retaining the association with Weymouth and Portland.)

In May 1895 he joined *HMS Alexandra*, Flagship of the Reserve Fleet at Portsmouth. *Alexandra*, launched in 1875 by the Princess of Wales at Chatham, was the last class of capital ship to be built with steam and sail propulsion, the latter being insisted on by diehards on the Admiralty Board. In 1878, coincidentally she was off the Dardanelles supporting the Turks and deterring Russian aggression. Her guns were mounted centrally, below the upper deck, and so as soon as turret mountings, which could be trained through at least 90 degrees, came in she became outdated, and was thus relegated to coastguard reserve. But she was Albert's first ship with modern guns, and this would have been useful training for him.

In December 1895, he was appointed to *HMS Royal Sovereign*, the lead ship of that class, designed by the eminent Sir William White, and a forerunner of the later dreadnoughts. She had been built at Portsmouth Dockyard, commissioned in 1892, embodying revolutionary advances in firepower, armour and speed. She was 410 feet long, propelled by twin 3-cylinder triple expansion steam engines with a top speed of 15.7 knots. She could carry up to 800 tons of coal, and had a complement of 700 men. What a ship for a young man to join! She was Flagship of the Channel Fleet, had attended the opening of the Kiel Canal in 1895, and regularly participated in exercises off the south coast and to the west of Ireland.

In October 1896, aged 18, Albert was rated Ordinary Seaman, and signed on for a 12-year engagement. He had grown to five feet seven inches, and sported a tattoo of a sailor and cask on his right forearm. He would not draw his daily tot of rum though until he was 21. He continued to serve in *Royal Sovereign* until June 1897, when her whole ship's company paid off and commissioned the brand new pre-dreadnought *HMS Mars* at Portsmouth. *Mars* participated in the Fleet Review to mark Queen Victoria's Diamond Jubilee in 1897, and became part of the Channel Fleet. Albert was rated up to Able Seaman in October 1897, aged just 19, leaving *Mars* for his first shore posting in Portsmouth Barracks in January 1898.

He then had to undertake professional training in gunnery at *HMS Excellent* and torpedoes at *HMS Vernon* in Portsmouth. This lasted until October 1899 when he joined *HMS Juno*, a protected cruiser of the 11th Cruiser Squadron based in Ireland, probably at Cork then called Queenstown. *Juno* was armed with five 6-inch guns, six 4.7-inch guns, six 3-inch guns for use against torpedo boats, and three 18-inch torpedo tubes which would have been Albert's action station. *Juno* had a maximum speed of 20 knots; this was typical of ships of her time, with each new class gradually being capable of increased speed.

He remained in *Juno* for a year and then took passage out to Australia in *HMS Blake* to join *HMS Royal Arthur*, then Flagship of the Australia Station. She acted as an escort to the Royal Yacht *Ophir*, the ship which carried the future King George V on his Empire tour. We know nothing special of his activities out there, but pleasant they must have been, with visits to the many British islands in the Pacific. Albert advanced his career, being first uprated to Leading Seaman, in which rank he would take charge of small parties of seamen and the ship's boats. He was then made up to Acting Petty Officer (Plate 23), giving him increased responsibilities and entitling him to become a member of the smaller and more comfortable Senior Rates Mess, but still sleeping in a hammock. This was good but not exceptional advancement. When *Royal Arthur* returned to the UK, he joined *HMS Phoebe* for the first six months of 1904, finally returning to England in *HMS Ringarooma* which arrived home at the end of November of that year. All these vessels in Australia were cruisers, but smaller and carrying less armour than *Juno*. They had two tall yellow funnels, white superstructure and black hulls. Grey paint for warships was not yet thought of! Now aged 26, Albert came home to Bridport for Christmas that year after four years away.

In 1905 he undertook further torpedo training at *HMS Vernon*, before joining the pre-dreadnought Canopus class *HMS Goliath* in the Channel and Home Fleets. To give you an idea of the size of these ships, *Juno*, although classed as a protected cruiser, was 350 feet in length, *Royal Arthur*, a similar class, was 387 feet, *Phoebe* smaller at 280 feet, and *Goliath*, surprisingly, only 390 feet. Albert's time in *Goliath* would have enabled him to get home on leave from time to time, but was otherwise notable only for his confirmation as

Petty Officer. He left *Goliath* in April 1909, thence back to *Vernon* for three months further training in torpedoes, followed by short periods in two protected cruisers, *Terrible* and *Argonaut*, in Home Waters.

In September 1910, he said goodbye to England once again, and joined the sloop, *HMS Espiegle* in the Persian Gulf (Plate 24). She was the last ship in the Navy to be built with a figurehead; the original has been saved and restored and is now on display in the Naval Museum at Portsmouth. There were six similar ships in this class of sloops, built to patrol the outposts of the Empire. They were 200 feet in length, 940 tons, and armed with six guns, two of which were mounted on the foc'sle. Originally they were rigged as barques or barquentines as well as having two screws, but the total loss with all hands of *HMS Condor* (one of an earlier class of similar design) off Vancouver Island whilst under sail, caused the Admiralty to abandon the sailing rig. However, *Espiegle,* although looking like a rich man's yacht, was never so rigged. She stood by off Port Arthur during the Russo-Japanese war 1904-05, ready to rescue any threatened British citizens. She moved to the Gulf soon after the war ended, ready to protect the increasingly important oil wells at Abadan. This was where Albert spent much time, with only awnings and any breeze as protection from the intense summer heat. For his pains, he was subsequently awarded the new 1915 Naval General Service Medal, Persian Gulf, for 'operations against Pirates, Gun Runners, and Slavers'. He therefore preceded others from Dorset who were to lose their lives fighting against the Turks in this area in the war. He took passage home in *HMS Gibraltar* and once more reached England in time to celebrate Christmas 1912 in Bridport.

After a short time in Portsmouth Barracks, he was appointed to *HMS Fisgard*, a Victorian hulk in Portsmouth Harbour used as a platform on which to train Engineers and Artificers. Such training on board ship at each UK Main Naval Base was instituted by Admiral Fisher from 1903 as he was concerned that the Navy would otherwise fall behind Germany in technical expertise. It is not clear whether Albert was employed to instruct technical ratings in basic seamanship, or whether, as is more likely, he himself was being taught basic electrical skills, a responsibility of the Torpedo Branch until 1946.

It was during his time in *Fisgard* that he married Susanna Gale in Powerstock Church on 3rd February 1913. The Gale family had lived in Nettlecombe for several years, after moving from Puddletown where Susanna was born in 1876. Her father was a journeyman carpenter; Susanna went into service and worked for a time in Onslow Square in London, and at Frampton. We do not know how they met, but after marrying, their home was with her family in Nettlecombe where their son William, their only child, was born on 21st March 1914. A month later, with an Irish Civil War appearing more likely than a European war, Albert joined the armoured cruiser *HMS Black Prince.* We know that he was paying his wife a weekly allotment of 31 shillings a week, which included a separation allowance of 11 shillings.

Black Prince and *Duke of Edinburgh* were armoured cruisers of the same class, completed in 1906. In addition, the First Cruiser Squadron contained two newer and slightly superior armoured cruisers, *Defence*, the Flagship, and *Warrior* (not to be confused with the first ironclad, now restored and moored at the entrance to Portsmouth Naval Museum). They were all part of the Mediterranean Fleet based in Malta which also comprised three battle cruisers, a squadron of light cruisers, and a couple of destroyer flotillas.

Black Prince (Plate 25) had been built by Thames Ironworks and laid down on 3rd June 1903. She was of nearly 14,000 long tons when fully loaded with fuel and ammunition. Measuring 505 feet in length, with a beam of 73 feet and a draught of 27 feet, she was propelled by two shafts from four triple expansion steam engines, driven by 20 water tube boilers and six cylindrical boilers, giving her a maximum speed of 23 knots. She was coal fuelled, but oil was sprayed on the coal to produce greater heat, and hence increased speed. She needed four funnels to disperse the smoke from the large number of boilers.

Her main armament was six 9.2-inch guns in single turrets, one for'ard, one aft, and two each side midships. Secondary armament was 6-inch guns, four in casemates on the main deck, and six on the upper deck; the four in casemates could not be fired when there was a sea running, and in 1916 these were relocated near the funnels on the upper deck. Finally she had 20 Vickers three-pounders, six of which were on the gun turrets, and 14 round the superstructure. She was also armed with three 18-inch torpedo tubes, which were fired from below the waterline; these would have been Albert's action station. Her complement was some 760 men. To provide some protection against enemy gunfire, there were two belts of steel between 3-inches and 6-inches thick along both sides of her hull, her decks were between 0.75-inch and 1.5-inches thick, gun turrets 4.5-inches-7-inches, and conning tower 10 inches thick. Some weight!

As July 1914 came to an end, and a European war seemed more and more likely, the Admiralty gave Admiral Sir Berkeley Milne, the Commander-in-Chief of the Mediterranean Fleet, orders that his first task was to escort the passage of units of the French Army from North Africa to France. Milne had been appointed by Churchill, First Lord of the Admiralty, against the advice of the Sea Lords, and events soon proved their judgment to have been correct. He was also informed that Germany had detached the battlecruiser *Göben* and cruiser *Breslau* from the High Seas Fleet in the north, and that they were heading for the Mediterranean, their exact purpose and destination unknown. It will be recalled from Chapter 6, they were to be sighted, and watched.

As the British Fleet headed towards Algeria to support the movement of French troops, they passed the two German ships heading east, but could do no more than exchange identities, as war had still not been declared. Two days later it was and it became important to find *Göben* and *Breslau*. Milne therefore sent his four armoured cruisers under Rear Admiral Ernest Troubridge to guard the entrance to the Adriatic in case the German intent was to link with the Austrians. Albert was thus facing the possibility of action within a week of the beginning of war, as *Black Prince* headed for the seas to the west of Corfu. The two German ships were next located coaling in neutral Messina in Sicily, their intent still not known. When they sailed from Messina they headed north-east, as though to make for the Adriatic, and Troubridge thus headed to cut them off. But in the dark, the Germans altered course to pass south of Greece; they were fortunately spotted by the light cruiser *Gloucester* which continued to trail them, and signalled Troubridge with their course and speed. Troubridge's ships were in a position to be able to intercept the Germans and he could have brought them to action. He initially sought to do this, and the excitement in the four British cruisers must have been great. But Troubridge began to vacillate, and in discussions with Captain Wray of *Defence*, eventually decided to abandon the pursuit because he judged the Germans to be a 'superior force', and his orders were not to engage such. (His decision contrasts with that of Commodore Harwood who, in 1939, successfully brought the much better armed *Graf Spee* to action with three smaller British cruisers). *Göben* and *Breslau* thus proceeded unmolested to Turkey where they became units of the Turkish Fleet and helped bring Turkey into the war on the side of Germany. Troubridge was summoned home and court martialled on board *HMS Bulwark*, at Portland, the ship in which Stoker Travers was serving – another co-incidence in this story. Troubridge, to great public disgust, was acquitted on the grounds that he obeyed the orders he had been given.

After the failure to stop *Göben* and *Breslau*, the First Cruiser Squadron was divided, with *Defence* and *Warrior* going to Gibraltar and West Africa, and *Black Prince* and *Duke of Edinburgh* to the Red Sea, with orders to protect any British convoys bringing troops from India to Europe, and to seize any German merchantmen they might find. On August 15th, *Black Prince* was in luck, falling upon the German ship *Sudmark,* 5113 tons, which, although built by Doxfords in Sunderland in 1913, belonged to the Hamburg Amerika line and was used on their Indian Ocean services. She was on passage from Colombo to Antwerp, possibly unaware of hostilities, otherwise she would have been better advised to take the longer route home round the Cape of Good Hope. She was escorted by *Black Prince* to Port Suez, where a prize crew was placed on board, whence she was sailed round to Alexandria. It is likely that Albert was a member of this prize crew, as in 1923 his wife was awarded on his behalf the sum of £54 as prize money. The delay in making this payment was because an appeal was made alleging that *Sudmark*'s seizure contravened the conditions of the Suez Canal Convention of 1880, to which Britain and Germany *inter alia* were signatories. The case was not decided until 1917, when the Appeal Court of the Privy Council rejected the appeal, and *Sudmark's* seizure as a prize was declared legal. *Black Prince* also captured another Hamburg Amerika vessel, *Istria*, but we know no more than that. In November 1914, any danger from German warships in the Red Sea was deemed unlikely, so *Black Prince* and *Duke of Edinburgh* returned to the UK where they arrived before Christmas, joining the other two ships and becoming part of the Home Fleet.

It may be helpful at this point to summarise Naval Policy against the German High Seas Fleet in the North Sea – or German Ocean as they preferred to call it. By treaty agreement, the French Navy took care of the Mediterranean, enabling the British to concentrate their forces around the UK, to protect both sides of the English Channel and the North Sea. At Harwich under Tyrwhitt, there were light cruisers, in the Forth, under Beatty, battle cruisers and the latest post dreadnought battleships, some more battleships at Invergordon in the Cromarty Firth, and the main Grand Fleet under Jellicoe at Scapa Flow in the Orkney Isles. Germany concentrated her fleet at the mouth of the Elbe and Jade rivers, to the north of Hamburg. Wireless communication was in its infancy, and thus unreliable, so that ships at sea communicated by flags, semaphore and morse signal lamps. Whilst ship design and capability had changed out of all recognition since Nelson's time, communication between ships had advanced very little. Nelson commanded 27 ships of the line and six smaller ships at Trafalgar, each moving at about three or four knots. Jellicoe had under his command at Jutland about 150 ships (40 battleships and battle cruisers, 30 cruisers, and 80 destroyers) each capable of steaming at over 20 knots. Not until the D-Day and Philippines landings in 1944 was there to be such a concentration of warships.

Other new weapons had become available in recent years. Firstly the mine – so a fleet had to beware of being lured into a minefield by an enemy. Secondly, the torpedo – fired mainly by fast moving small ships, closing capital ships under cover of smoke screens or darkness, to which the main defence was to build capital ships with anti-torpedo bulges below their waterline such that they could sustain a hit. Thirdly, the submarine – slow moving but at this time undetectable when submerged. The response to this was for capital ships to steam a zig-zag course at reasonably high speed so that the slow moving submarine found it difficult to aim accurately at his target. Mines and submarines had sunk or damaged many ships in the Dardanelles, and this lesson was foremost in Jellicoe's mind.

The Grand Fleet outnumbered and could outgun the German High Seas Fleet, and its ships were generally capable of higher speed. The German ships possessed better gunfire control. They had Zeppelins for reconnaissance, as opposed to seaplanes based on converted cross channel ferry steamers that could only operate in calmer seas. As it turned out, the German warships were of superior hull construction.

Once war had started, German policy was to make forays with cruisers towards the English coast, with capital ships in support but out of view. They had succeeded in bombarding towns on the East Coast, but always withdrew without loss before facing any British force. They were caught by Beatty with his battle cruisers at the Dogger Bank, inflicting damage but losing their battleship *Blücher* as they retreated to the safety of the Jade.

For the Grand Fleet and Albert in *Black Prince*, the war had been without real incident from 1914 until Jutland in 1916. They headed out into the North Sea many times on seemingly never ending patrols if ever there was the slightest chance of the German Fleet being brought to action. Continuous weapon training was the order of the day, interspersed with recreation ashore near their base, and leave probably only when ships dry-docked or needed repairs. Albert was fortunate in this respect when *Black Prince* had her secondary armament modified, giving him time to return home and see his wife and young boy William.

May 30th, 1916, dawned as another typical day in harbour off Invergordon. Albert had received a letter from home the day before, so we surmise that he remained on board to write a reply, whilst many of the ship's company went ashore to play football or golf, or walk in the hills to the north. The pencil, handwritten original version has been kept, and is today in the possession of his granddaughter. Much faded, it does not lend itself to reproduction, but the words can be made out and it reads as follows:

HMS Black Prince
c/o GPO London
30th May 1916

My Darling Wife and Babe,

I now take the greatest of pleasure in writing a few lines to you both in answer to your most kind and ever loving letter which I was so pleased to receive yesterday, to know that both you, my own, and darling babe were quite alright and enjoying the best of health again, and that Mother (probably his wife's mother) and Bess (his sister) are alright. Well, my darling girl I am very pleased to tell you that I am enjoying the best of health at present. We are going on quite alright, not very busy now, just keeping fit and ready for anything that may happen, and waiting for the news that we are coming down for a few days. I don't think it will be much longer before we shall hear something definite and I am so longing to come down and see you and the bonny babe once again.

I should very much liked to have been with you when you went to the top of the hill [possibly Eggardon. Ed.]. I'll bet it was lovely and I am sure you all enjoyed yourselves. No wonder babe was tired. He has not been up there before has he? I should like to have seen him between you and Bess, going up like a little man, and to have heard his baby-talk. But it won't be much longer before I will be there with you (from this and previous remarks he was obviously expecting some leave – perhaps the ship was due for a dry docking or boiler clean).

I see you and Mother have been getting in coal. I should like to have seen you after you had finished! (don't laugh). I am pleased that you are having some nice weather and I hope that it will be nice when I come down, a storm now and then will do no end of good to bring the gardens on. We are having some nice weather, a little chilly during the night, but lovely and sunny during the day. We have started to leave off our winter clothing. Well, dearest, I shall not be sending on any note the first of this month as I might want some for travelling and you never know what you might require.

I have two or three little things to bring down this time, but it won't be very heavy. I won't forget babe's sweets.

Well now my own darling girl, I don't think I have any more to say this time, so give my love to Bess and Mother, give babe a few kisses for me and look well after yourself and bonny babe.

Goodnight darling, God bless you all and keep you safe,

from your loving Albert.

The calm was not to last, for the Admiralty had become increasingly suspicious over the previous days at unusual German submarine movements without any attacks on merchant ships. They learnt too that Admiral Scheer, the Fleet Commander, had moved from shore to his Flagship, *SMS Friedrich der Grosse.* At 17.16 on 30th, the Admiralty sent a telegraphed message to Jellicoe and to Beatty ordering them to raise steam, and at 17.40 a further message saying "Germans intend some operations commencing tomorrow morning....you should concentrate to eastward of Long Forties ready for eventualities". Boats scurried ashore with mail, returning with men from recreation whilst smoke soon started pouring from the funnels of all ships in harbour.

At 22.20 *Black Prince*, under the command of recently appointed Captain T.P. Bonham, started shortening in her anchor cable, to be ready to proceed with the other three armoured cruisers at 22.30. Rear Admiral Sir Richard Arbuthnot, flying his Flag in *Defence*, then took his cruisers to sea, ahead of the eight dreadnoughts and the destroyers, heading for the rendezvous with Jellicoe and the Grand Fleet from Scapa at first light on the morning of May 31st, 100 miles to the east. Beatty, meanwhile had slipped out of the Forth, heading for his planned rendezvous with Jellicoe later that afternoon.

Scheer had similarly sent Admiral Hipper with his battle cruisers and light cruisers ahead of the main German Fleet. At 14.28 Beatty's leading light cruiser *Galatea* sighted and opened fire on Hipper's cruisers, and before long both battle cruiser fleets were in action. Ships on both sides were damaged but Beatty had two of his battle cruisers blown up when struck by German fire.

This was the scene when Arbuthnot with his armoured cruisers, about 16 miles ahead of Jellicoe, came into sight. He first saw the badly damaged German cruiser *Wiesbaden*, and determined to take his squadron closer to finally sink her. He did not appreciate that the German battle cruisers were so close, and was thus surprised when he came under heavy fire from them. Their fire was accurate – *Defence* took a mortal hit and blew up with the loss of all hands, *Warrior* was badly damaged. *Black Prince* and *Duke of Edinburgh*, 16 and 8 miles respectively to starboard of *Defence* were forced to turn away to avoid approaching British battle cruisers and they then withdrew to the north towards the safety of Jellicoe's capital ships.

What now happened to *Black Prince* is not clear. There are scraps of evidence, none corroborated, so I will piece together to the best of my knowledge what I think took place. I suspect *Black Prince* was damaged because one report is that she was capable only of 12 knots. After withdrawing from 'Windy Corner', the area where *Defence* blew up, she sighted the Grand Fleet manoeuvring to engage Scheer, and kept clear, whilst attempting to rectify damage to her hull and armament. In the North Sea gloom, smoke and then dusk, she lost sight of the main fleet, but limped southwards, assuming that this was the direction in which the Grand Fleet would head. At 20.45 *Black Prince* signalled that she had sighted a German submarine, but gave no position, so this information is unhelpful, other than giving rise to a view that she might have been sunk by the submarine.

After Scheer had broken off the battle, and also disappeared in the fading light, Jellicoe determined to head south and place himself between Scheer and his base in the Jade, puzzling over which of the two routes home he might take. During the night Scheer slowed to enable his damaged ships to keep up, and in so doing actually fell behind Jellicoe, and crossed astern of Jellicoe without being sighted by any British ships. Except *Black Prince* – who sighted what she hoped was the British Fleet only to find that they were the enemy. She engaged the German battleship *Rheinland* at 23.35, scoring two hits with her 6-inch guns, before receiving an enormous broadside from three or four more German battleships, including Scheer's flagship, *Friedrich der Grosse,* each battleship illuminating *Black Prince* with their searchlights at a range of only half a mile. We doubt *Black Prince* managed to score any more hits on her adversaries, such was her surprise, but with two of her four funnels demolished, and fires raging the whole length of the ship, the Germans soon landed a shot on her magazines. She blew up with a great flash, and all onboard perished. These details from German sources did not come to light until after the war, although the British destroyer *Spitfire,* recovering from ramming a German cruiser, did tell of an unknown vessel with two funnels, fires raging throughout the ship, blowing up at about midnight.

Black Prince's sinking, whether by gunfire or submarine torpedo, was not established until Germany issued reports of a great victory as soon as Scheer returned to harbour. These reports reached England before the Admiralty was able to respond with the British version of events, but there was huge disbelief at home that the Navy could have lost so many ships. In Nettlecombe, with only the worst news coming through, Albert's family must have been distraught, and were kept in suspense for several days. It was not until 7th June 1916, that his wife received a standard letter from the Accountant General of the Navy, informing her that Albert was believed to have been on board *Black Prince* when she was sunk in action and must be presumed to have lost his life. The next day, the bells of Powerstock Church were tolled in his memory. She also received a standard letter signed by First Sea Lord, Arthur Balfour, stating that *"The King commands me to assure you of the true sympathy of His Majesty and The Queen in your sorrow"*. On 5th May 1919, she was awarded a War Gratuity of a single payment of £13.

Susanna was thus left to bring up their son on her own, with little by way of pension. Her war widow's pension in 1920 amounted to 46s 8d per week. She continued to live with her parents in Nettlecombe for a number of years, eventually moving to a house in New Road, Uploders where she died in 1959. Son William served an apprenticeship with the local builders Barretts as a carpenter, like his maternal grandfather. He married Vera Knight on 24th September 1936, lived in Bradpole and served for many years as organist at Loders Church. His was a reserved occupation, and he was unable to join the Navy as war again came closer in 1939, but eventually served in London with the Grenadier Guards. William died in 1985.

Ian Berry

On a personal note, I have been much moved by many similarities between Albert's life and my own. Some 60 years after him, I had volunteered as a Boy Seaman. Like him I did some of my initial training in a newer HMS Howe at Devonport, and then at Portland. Whilst serving in HMS Crossbow we were based for a NATO exercise at Moudros in the North Aegean, the same town on Lemnos used as a support base for Gallipoli. His Naval General Service medal was awarded with the clasp 'Persian Gulf'; mine, the same medal and ribbon, but awarded with a clasp 'Near East'. And finally, 60 years apart, ships in which we were serving were both sunk in the North Sea, not 100 miles distant from each other – his in war action in darkness, mine in a peacetime accidental collision which I had the good fortune to survive. Ironically, I was in a ship heading for a Squadron goodwill visit to Hamburg!

CHAPTER 12

Charles Watts
15ᵗʰ Battalion The Hampshire Regiment
Died First Battle of the Somme, 7th October 1916

CHARLIE WATTS was among the several Powerstock men whose final years are probably irrecoverable. Yet in a sense, he had a very representative war. He died not in any unusual theatre but on the Western Front, and he was twenty-three years old.

Charlie was the fifth son of William Watts, originally of Shroton, and Eliza Cross of Winterbourne Stickland. They had married in 1877, when William was described as a journeyman shoemaker. The census of 1881 shows the shoemaker at Child Okeford with his growing family but by 1885 the couple had come to Powerstock where their second daughter Blanche and all subsequent children were born. William now worked as a gamekeeper on the Hooke estate, based on the farmhouse at Grays (Plate 26), east across the fields from Wytherston, and it was there in April 1892 that Charlie was born. He followed his older brothers to the school at Toller, a good deal nearer than Powerstock, which he left in March 1907. Four years later he was working as a grocer's assistant in Bridport, and by the time war broke out he appears to have moved to Portsmouth where he joined up in the second of the Pals battalions formed by a local committee in the town in the spring of 1915. All the famed comradeship and neighbourliness of the Pals Battalions would have been lost on 21627 Charles Watts, unless he had been in the town for some time and did indeed join up with his pals. His training exposed him to the complexities and the huge scale of the great volunteer army being assembled during the ensuing months as he was moved in training first to Aldershot and then to Marlborough, but he was still relatively near Dorset. His older brothers had meanwhile all joined up, each in different regiments including not only the Somerset Light Infantry, but the Durham Light Infantry and the Royal Garrison Artillery. In May 1916 the Second Portsmouth

Plate 25. *HMS Black Prince* - Leaving Portland Harbour 1907
from a watercolour by Alma Claude Burlton Cull.

Plate 26. The Watts' farmhouse at Grays Farm. Seated in front are RNAS aircrew
and members of the airship ground-handling team, autumn 1918. The officers found
accommodation here and on neighbouring farms. The ratings were accommodated in bell
tents at this, the Toller Porcorum outstation, one of a number on the south coast responsible
for anti-submarine warfare from the Western Approaches and through the Channel.

Plate 27. The Sea Scout Zero (SSZ) single-engined airship. It was powered by a 75 hp Rolls Royce pusher giving a top speed of 53 mph. Armament comprised two 110 lb bombs or one 230-250 lb bomb with a Lewis machine gun in the forward position. In Dorset, SSZ Class airships operated from both Toller and Upton. Their open cockpits allowed an excellent view for crews searching out U-boats but warm protective clothing was essential.

Plate 28. Pte Richard Reed (right) when serving in the Dorset Regiment.

Plate 29. Richard Reed's temporary grave. Plates 28 & 29 © Brenda Sharp

Plate 30. Leo and Brenda Sharp lay flowers at the memorial for Richard Reed in Powerstock Church.

Plate 31. E.F.A. Stone standing, W.C.P. Stone sitting.

Photographs of the unfortunate Sapper William Stone RE. Believed to have been wounded in action whilst serving in the Nairobi Signals Unit. Casualty evacuated to the Military Hospital in Poona to recuperate. He died of Spanish 'Flu whilst in hospital.

Plates 31, 32 & 40 kindly provided by the late Mrs V. Stone of Bournemouth.

, friends."
RUGG.—Oct. 14, at the Cobb, Lyme Regis, Mary Anna, wife of G. A. Rugg, aged 31.
STONE.—Died Oct. 5, 1918, at Poona, India, Sapper W. Stone, aged 24 years, eldest son of Mr. E. O. Stone, Powerstock, and fiancé of Miss Emily Rendall, Symondsbury.
    "There is a link death cannot sever—
    ~ Love and remembrance last for ever."
WILLIAMS.—Oct. 25, at Plenty House, Whitchurch Canonicorum, Grace Gwendoline, eldest daughter of the Rev. J. Williams.

Bridport News, late October 1918

Plate 32. Sapper William Stone.

Plate 33. *HMS Carlisle.*

THOSE WHOSE NAMES ARE
HONOURED HERE LIE BURIED
ELSEWHERE IN SIBERIA
THEIR NAME LIVETH
FOR EVERMORE

ROYAL NAVY
J/51017 (DEV) ABLE SEAMAN A. E. J. BREWER 5.11.1918
K/40777 STOKER 1ST CLASS G. BRITTON 14.7.1918
CHAPLAIN THE REV. W. L. FORD 9.5.1918
J/20280 (DEV) ABLE SEAMAN T. HOWARTH 29.4.1918
K/1471G STOKER PETTY OFFICER H. MARSH 22.10.1919
297225 LEADING STOKER D. J. SMITH 24.3.1919

ROYAL MARINE LIGHT INFANTRY
PO/20028 PRIVATE W. H. REED 9.9.1919

ROYAL NAVAL RESERVE
3567/51 STOKER S. MANSON 18.2.1919

ROYAL FIELD ARTILLERY
LIEUTENANT COLONEL E. A. STEEL DSO 14.10.1918

ROYAL ENGINEERS
CAPTAIN C. K. DIGBY-JONES 5.9.1918

HAMPSHIRE REGIMENT
355728 PRIVATE L. R. BURT 29.5.1919
355186 SERJEANT C. A. LAWES 22.1.1919
39771 PRIVATE A. MAY 18.9.1918
39628 PRIVATE W. M. TAYLOR 30.7.1919

MIDDLESEX REGIMENT
G/99184 PRIVATE G. W. CROSSLEY 17.12.1919
F/208200 PRIVATE J. FULLER 16.1.1919
G/43205 PRIVATE G. HARDING 20.11.1918
J9629 PRIVATE E. C. WADE 6.9.1919
G/33294 SERJEANT S. J. WEBB 3.3.1919

CANADIAN INFANTRY
77103 PRIVATE E. BIDDLE 2.10.1919
2760750 RIFLEMAN H. L. BUTLER 17.10.1919
19773 RIFLEMAN

Plate 34.
Memorial to British and Empire Forces who died in Siberia. Stoker Petty Officer Harry Marsh was killed almost a year after the Armistice.

CWGC

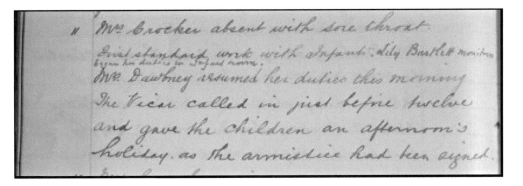

Plate 35. Extract from Powerstock School Register. 'The Vicar called in just before twelve and gave the children an afternoon's holiday as the armistice had been signed.'

Plate 36.
Reverend William Rickman,
Vicar of Powerstock 1906-1924.

Plate 37.
Captain Charles Lloyd Sanctuary MC
died 15 November 1916.

Plate 38. A return to normal duties. The bellringers of Powerstock.

Plate 39. The Christmas Truce 1914. German soldiers of the 134th Saxon Regiment photographed by the donor with men of the Royal Warwickshire Regiment in No Man's Land on the Western Front. ©IWM (HU035801)

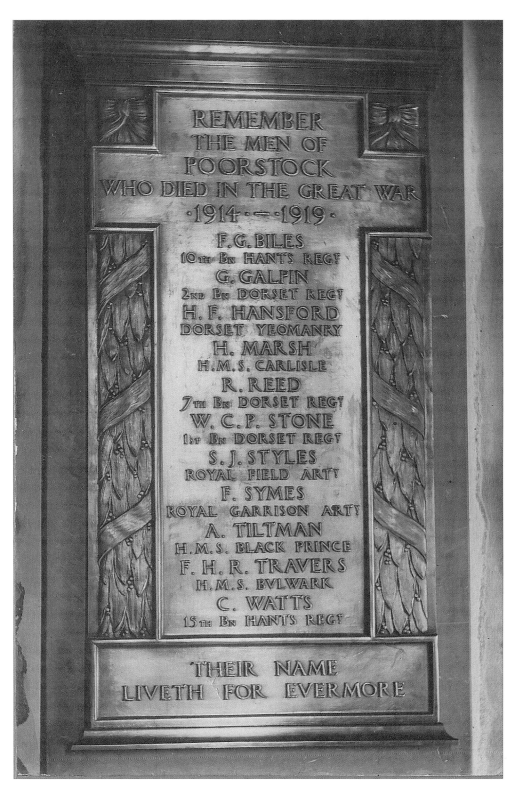

Plate 40

PLACES THEY KNEW

A visit today to places well known to parishioners 100 years ago. Clockwise from top:
The Marquis of Lorne pub, Nettlecombe. The Square, Powerstock (Reading Room on left,
used during the war for club meetings and lectures). Powerstock School. The 4000 year old
Eggardon Bronze Age Fort (the Dorsets would detrain at Powerstock Station at the bottom of
the hill as a preliminary to attacking the fort. Nothing could be more guaranteed to empty the
school). 12th century Church of St Mary the Virgin. The Three Horseshoes pub, Powerstock.

Pals, now part of the 122$^{nd.}$ Brigade of the 41st Division, made their way to France.

The long line of the Western Front that had taken shape in the last months of 1914 stretched in a great curve across France and Belgium, from Artois in the north-west towards the prominent town of Verdun 200 miles to the south-east. Defence against German attack was shared between British and French commanders, without either one being supreme. By 1916 the British Army was commanded by Douglas Haig, but in a complex relationship with Joseph Joffre commanding the French. There was little doubt that the clinching victory over the German Army would only be achieved on the Western Front, and the failure of 'sideshows' like the assault at Gallipoli in Turkey the previous year made this all the more obvious. But, as the French came under massive attack at Verdun in the spring of 1916, preparations for this onslaught became distorted and more hurried. A decision was made to mount a massive attack where the British and French armies met, on either side of the River Somme. This was Joffre's suggestion, and the timing – the attack was to take place at the end of June - was dictated because Joffre felt the French army could not hold out indefinitely at Verdun.

During the early months of 1916 the massive British Army was assembled on the Somme. To a very large extent this was an army of volunteers, young men who had joined up in the fervour of enthusiastic patriotism in response to Kitchener's famous poster 'Your Country Need You'. They were hurriedly trained, but the battle planners realised that this was too inexperienced an army to execute complicated manoeuvres, and in addition each was going to be loaded with heavy packs of kit.

Briefly, the plan was to destroy the German lines, and the barbed wire defending them, with a colossal preliminary bombardment, and then the infantry battalions would go over the top of their own trenches and advance across no man's land, hopefully assisted by a barrage of artillery organised to keep just in front of them. If all went well, and the German trenches were taken, this would then be followed up by cavalry that might be able to reach Bapaume fifteen miles away to the north-east, by nightfall. The First Battle of the Somme was the last time horse cavalry was used on a large scale in Western Europe.

Many factors combined to ensure that the actual outcome was very different. The first day of the Battle of the Somme saw the greatest losses ever sustained by British forces in one day – approximately 60,000 men – 19,000 dead. On much of the front, almost no ground was gained. The bombardment did not shatter the German trenches – they were too deep and too solidly built for that. Neither did it, in many areas, destroy the barbed wire. Haig had ordered the area of the bombardment to be doubled in depth of coverage, so that it was insufficiently concentrated, and in any case the shells were frequently of poor quality and failed to explode. The Germans were able to survive the bombardment and their machine guns mowed down the British, walking towards them. The northern half of the British line gained almost nothing, but on the section nearest the French the armies had advanced about one mile. The 'First Day of the Somme' has achieved bitter notoriety, but it was by no means the end of a battle that lasted 141 days. The terrible losses continued, even if never quite of the intensity of the first day. Between 15th July and 14th September there took place almost continuously, attack and counter-attack; two miles of ground were gained, at the cost of 82,000 casualties. When the First Battle of the Somme ended on 1st November, the British had lost 420,000, the French 195,000 and the Germans 650,000. The high German figure arose as a result of counter-attacks in which irreplaceable junior non-commissioned officers were lost. The Medical Services could not cope with injuries of this magnitude, the consequence of which was the death of a high proportion of the wounded.

Arriving in France in May the Hampshires had had their baptism of fire up near Ypres at Ploegsteert (called Plugstreet by the British), and had then been called down to that part of the Somme front where the British had made their most significant advance on the first day of the battle, close to where the Battalion fought side by side with the French. On 15th September, a significant attack took place aiming through the village of Flers towards the fortified village of Gueudecourt, in which the Hampshires played a leading part together with New Zealand troops deployed for the first time in the battle. The attack is significant because of the deployment of eighteen tanks (Mark I), for the first time. Although several had engine failure, tanks were effective, not least in terrifying the German defenders, and the engagement provided useful experience before the use of tanks in much larger concentrations later in the war.

The Hampshires' attack was very successful, within the diminishing expectations of what advance was possible: about 2000 yards were gained, but this was achieved at the cost of eleven officers and nearly 300 men killed or wounded. The battalion was too weakened to fight again till the first few days in October when they fought a series of vicious and small-scale battles near the village of Gueudecourt until 9th October when they were relieved and withdrew to Mametz.

On that day, 9th October, Charlie Watts died of his wounds. Because he did not actually die in battle, it is impossible to know at what stage in the five months since his arrival in France he had received his wounds. Similarly, there is no record of when he was promoted to Lance-Corporal, and so second in command of the section, which brought with it a slight increase in pay. For the Hampshires, the Battle of Flers lasted little more than a day and, apart from that, the battalion seems to have been under enemy fire for about ten weeks. Along with over 70,000 British and French soldiers whose grave is unknown, Charlie is commemorated on the Thiepval memorial. This masterpiece by Sir Edwin Lutyens, one of the finest memorials ever to be erected, stands no more than five miles west of Flers where Charlie Watts was perhaps most likely to have received his wound. His name is on a corner of one of the four great inner piers that surround the 'Stone of Remembrance'. Implicitly also, he may be commemorated by the memorial at Flers to the 41st Division, of which the 15th Hampshires formed a part.

It was not until April 1917 that Powerstock's Parish Magazine was able to offer condolence to Charlie Watts's parents, to whom the news of his death had only just been delivered. Visitors to the Electric Palace cinema in Bridport at the end of the previous October had been able to see for themselves the 'Enormous Attraction' of the film of the Somme battle, 'taken while the fighting was actually in progress'. 'The film is probably the most wonderful war picture that has ever been exhibited   …calculated to still further increase the admiration which everyone feels for the bravery of our soldiers who are fighting for our country on the battlefield… The dauntless courage of the British Tommy is vividly portrayed, and what is even more noticeable, his kindness to the defeated foe… These are the actions which help to make our fighting men the finest in the world. But as for the picture itself, it will be remembered as one of the remarkable achievements of the cinematograph.'

Perhaps, the upbeat, propagandistic tone may have done something to assuage those parents and friends to whom the wretched news would, as it did for the Watts family at Gray's Farm, eventually arrive. In 1918, their empty bedrooms were occupied by members of the RNAS aircrew from Drackenorth (Plate 27).

Tim Connor

Sources:
Royal Hampshire Regiment Museum, Serle's House, Winchester.
C.T.Atkinson, *The Royal Hampshire Regiment*, [1950 -55].
J.Keegan, *The Face of Battle* [1977]
J.P.Harris, *Douglas Haig and the First World War* [2008]

CHAPTER 13

Richard Reed
1st Battalion The Wiltshire Regiment
Died Flanders, 5th February 1917

ONE OF the surprising details to have arisen from the study of the memorial to the eleven men of Powerstock who died in the First World War, is that not all have any long claim to belong to the village. Quite how surprising that may be for the nation as a whole could only be known if and when every parish war memorial in Britain is studied in the same detail.

Richard Reed is a good example of this. He was born in 1877, the third son of John Richard and Emily Reed, of Ropley near Arlesford, Hants. His father was described as a farm labourer, and Richard, the son, also appears to have been drawn to the outdoor life. He is called a 'Groom, domestic' when he is mentioned on later censuses, working, along with a couple of other servants for a Mr Sydney Joliffe of Heath House, Sussex Road, Petersfield, for the ten years between 1901 and 1911. By 1911, he had moved down the road and set up house with his new wife, Helen Ruth (Young) whom he had married the previous year. Helen had been born in Stepney, and had previously been employed as a kitchen maid at Bighton, near Richard's home village of Ropley, to which she returned after her husband's death. At the beginning of the war, Richard appears to have been at Melplash, perhaps working as a groom at Melplash Court, and he enlisted at Bridport into the 7th Battalion, the Dorsetshire Regiment.The only photograph thought to be of Richard shows a couple of men wearing what could be the Dorsets' cap badge (Plate 28). By 1914 he would have been 37 years old; judging by a resemblance to his twin, Emily, of whom a fine photograph exists, he may be the man on the right.

At some stage after this Richard was transferred to the 1st Battalion, the Wiltshire Regiment, and he spent his final years with them. The Battalion was in France before the end of July 1914 and took part in the battles at Mons and Le Cateau as the great German offensive, intended to capture Paris and end the war in the west before Christmas, was held up and finally halted. Once that had been achieved, both British and German armies raced north-westwards in an attempt to outflank each other till they ended up at the Channel. The Wiltshires then took part in the first of several battles fought around the town of Ypres, in Belgium, defending individual farms or tiny strongholds. The regimental history describes the fighting only briefly, and is concerned mainly with commanding officers; other ranks scarcely get a look-in. The Battalion spent the entire war in one part of the Western Front or another, with periods of action alternating with rest or 'intensive training'. Perhaps Richard obtained some leave home, and so he may have seen his youngest daughter Marjorie, who was born in 1915.

The following year the Battalion, by now part of the 25th Division, took part in the Battle of the Somme, in which they were involved in the heart of the British sector in the attack on Thiepval. Only slight gains were achieved at great cost. After the main attack in July, slow, damaging small-scale operations continued along most of the front, but only on the southern end was any significant advance achieved. In October, just as the next push was planned at Flers, the Wiltshires were ordered north again. The front was by now so established that different parts of it were linked by special railway lines, well behind the front line. This was just one aspect of the industrialisation of warfare: enormous numbers of men could be delivered to a particular part of the front with great speed, but after that, beyond the front line, advance could only take place on foot, and against murderous machine guns.

The Wiltshires detrained at Bailleul, just on the French side of the border, a few miles south-west of Ypres where they were again involved in the same trench warfare that they had fought for almost two years and at which they were by now considerable experts. The hope remained however that a breakthrough could somehow be achieved. This sort of warfare, where defence is more effective than attack, was to be reversed by the development of the tank, but only after its many mechanical weaknesses had been ironed out. The weeks passed in intensive training, in grenade throwing, or trench building, alternating with sports like football, cross-country running, boxing or a tug of war, and then fortnights of exposure at the front. Then the regiment would change places with the 10th Cheshires or the Loyal Lancashires, and return behind the lines. The enemy became a familiar presence, such that when a new regiment faced them, the regimental diarist commented that with the Saxon troops life was a good deal more relaxed. It was during one such period of duty at the front, when every day was described by the diarist as 'quiet', that Reed received his injury. The weather was very cold. The diarist described the day:

> "12 January 1917. A quiet day during which the usual work of repairing trenches continued. There were two casualties 10468 Pte. HUGHES,W. ('C' Coy.) killed, and 26672 Pte, READ (sic), R. wounded".

Reed must have been evacuated to a field hospital, if only because, when he died three weeks later, the regimental diary does not mention the fact. But the news came back to his family relatively quickly, for by April the *Powerstock Parish Magazine* – for the only time such a mention is made in the surviving numbers of the magazine – extended condolence for two of the village's war casualties, one of which reads:

> "We would like to express our deep sympathy...with Mrs. Richard Reed of Mappercombe, in the loss of her husband who died of wounds in France last February".

This is the only reference that ties Richard Reed, a Hampshire man, to Powerstock. Perhaps Richard and Helen Reed had recently moved their family from Melplash to take up the post of Groom for the wife of Captain Hugh Nicholson, who was himself still with his regiment in France.

Richard was buried in the cemetery at Bailleul, one white headstone amid countless others in the immaculate war cemeteries across the Western Front, and now surrounded with modern housing. Far more poignant is the faded sepia photograph of the temporary cross marking his place of burial, (Plate 29) before the War Cemetery was built, and which is preserved in the family. The granddaughter of his twin sister Emily, Mrs Brenda Sharp had done much to assemble material on her great uncle's war service, but until the Powerstock project was under way she had not been able to discover the place of his memorial. It is particularly fitting, therefore, that in March 2014, she was at last able to lay flowers by the memorial in Powerstock Church.

"I have visited his grave in Bailleul on the Belgian border near Ypres a number of times but always failed to find his name commemorated in England. I've looked in Portsmouth, Gosport, Ropley and even got as far as Melplash but without success – sadly, I had given up hope of ever finding it. Unfortunately, I don't have a photo of my great uncle, only one of my grandmother Emily Reed, his twin – the twins came ninth of a family of 15 children born. As a girl, I only knew an older great aunt who lived in a lovely Georgian house in Winchester. The one photo, though, that has always moved me to tears, is that of a temporary wooden marker of the preliminary and immediate mass grave of my great uncle. Those bodies remained in this grave until they were relocated later to the permanent site at Bailleul. All those young men – all those families like mine – so sad. I don't know what made me have another search on the internet as I really didn't expect to find anything, but when I typed in 'War Memorials in Dorset' to the search engine it suddenly felt so spooky to read the third entry in the list of names and the question: 'Has anyone got a photograph of Richard Reed?' I almost could not believe it after all these years. It has given me such joy to make this journey and Leo and I shall certainly be here for the Remembrance service in November. Thank you to everyone who has made this happen – what serendipity."

Keith Rixton
Retired Farmer

CHAPTER 14

William Charles Penny Stone
Royal Engineers
Died Poona, 5th October 1918

On February the 23rd 1892 two parish families were united in Powerstock church. Edmund Charles Stone, a Powerstock born farm worker, married Rhoda Legg, a net braider from Nettlecombe.

On April the 23rd 1894 they celebrated the birth of their first son, William Charles Penny, who was followed by Ernest Frederick Albert, born on August 15th 1895, and lastly Lily Florence Sarah Matilda who arrived in the spring of 1897. Sadly Lily, their only daughter, died later that same year.

In the 1901 census the family are to be found living in the Three Horse Shoes Inn Powerstock. One can only assume that they were victims of one of the many house and cottage fires that occurred in the Parish when so many of the houses were thatched and in very close proximity to one another. Perhaps they were staying at the pub whilst waiting to be re-housed. The one benefit of living in the pub, apart from it being one of the social hubs of the village, was its short walk to the village school, which the young William and Ernest were now attending.

Tragedy struck the young family once more, when in 1903 Rhoda Stone sadly died aged 35, leaving her husband to care for their two young sons, which would have been extremely difficult as his farm labouring would have meant an early start and a late finish combined with poor wages. Fortunately Rhoda's sister Ada came to the rescue and moved in with the family and kept house.

By 1911 Edmund, William, Ernest and Ada were living in Nettlecombe, Edmund still working on the land. William is listed as a domestic groom and, at the time, Ernest was unemployed. By 1912, aged 18, William must have wanted a career change or better pay as he left his job and joined the Dorchester based Dorset Regiment. It must have been at some point between joining the army and the time war was declared that William met Emily Rendall, a Bradpole born girl, three years his junior, now living in Symondsbury with her parents and three brothers. The two became engaged, but sadly there was to be no wedding as William did not come back from the war. If my research is correct, Emily found happiness once more and married in 1922.

When war was declared in August 1914, servicemen were urged to make a Will in case they were killed in action. William made his on 23rd August 1914. These Wills had to be validated by the War Office before they could be accepted. The validation of William's Will occurred a year after his death. The scrutineer was required to confirm the named person was in actual military service within the meaning of the Wills Act 1837 and that the document was recognised by the War Office as constituting a valid Will.

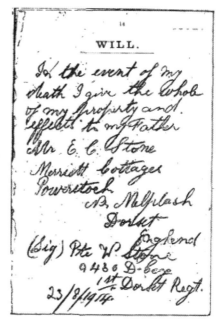

His family had returned to live in Powerstock by the outbreak of war. The constant change of addresses between Powerstock and Nettlecombe is not surprising as there were many farms in the area, and this being the era of horsepower, with mechanisation still fairly basic, many job opportunities on farms would have arisen. Some of the jobs would offer better pay, and some had better accommodation. Understandably his father changed employers to suit whichever need was deemed the most necessary for the good of the family.

At some stage in the war William Stone (Plates 31 & 32) was transferred to East Africa. The unification of Germany after the Franco-Prussian War had created an increasingly powerful nation resentful of the size of Britain's colonial empire. The more favoured areas of Africa had already been occupied and controlled by Britain and France. Germany followed suit and by 1884 had control of territories in West and Southwest Africa, and most importantly in East Africa, in what is now essentially Tanzania, Rwanda and Burundi. Prior to the outbreak of the Great War there had been some degree of understanding between the powers to exclude black Africa from any future conflict. In fact the German government seemed keener in maintaining neutrality than was the British. Neither the Governors of German East Africa nor of British Kenya had much appetite for aggression. This did not however prevent young settlers on both sides forming militia units in readiness for conflict. In August 1914, hostilities effectively started with a British warship shelling the German wireless station at Dar-es-Salaam, and a German cruiser operating in waters off Kenya sank a British vessel, thereafter successfully evading detection for almost a year before being sunk herself by a small naval force.

The developing campaign in East Africa was very different from that in Western Europe. There was no trench warfare. It was essentially a war of manoeuvre in the form of skirmishes between opposing sides and few large battles. A major threat to participants was disease, lack of food, and wild animals. Poor communications and equipment shortages were constant problems.

The German force mainly comprised well-trained black Askaris (soldier warriors) led by German officers and commanded by the legendary von Lettow-Vorbeck whose early successes led Britain to plan for a full scale military expedition against him. Two Brigades of British and Indian troops were sent out from India in November 1914 only to be repulsed and humiliated on the beaches, abandoning sufficient supplies and ammunition to sustain von Lettow-Vorbeck's campaign throughout 1915. More British troops arrived, a minor victory followed, which led the Germans hereon to pursue largely guerrilla tactics. In essence, the German strategy with their significantly smaller force was to draw substantial British and Indian resources of manpower and equipment into East Africa, which might otherwise have been deployed in Western Europe.

During 1916, fighting increased in intensity with the arrival of South African troops under General Smuts who had been Britain's adversary in the earlier Boer War. Smuts was given command of the Allied operation, and with now vastly superior numbers pursued a relentless campaign against von Lettow-Vorbeck who, until the Armistice in Europe, consistently avoided defeat in the enormous and challenging terrain of the African bush whilst destroying bridges and lines of communication. His success was in no small part due to the superior resistance of his African Askaris to many of the parasitic diseases that afflicted the Allied troops who experienced a high toll of sickness and death – 31 non-battle casualties to one in actual battle.

It is against this background that William Stone at some stage early in the war transferred from the Dorsetshires to the Royal Engineers, serving in what is described in the records as the Nairobi Signals Company. The First World War predated the formation of the Royal Signals. The role of Signals units in this period was to install and maintain telegraph lines, wireless and other signalling equipment in support of infantry and other forces. A specialised role related to intelligence operations. Signal intercepts of German radio transmissions had begun in Mombasa in 1913. Initially these were in clear but later coded.

Coded signals were then cabled to Bombay for overland transmission to Simla where they were decoded by Indian Army experts, with the results sent back to Nairobi. Eventually this work was carried out in Kenya itself. It has not been possible to establish precisely what William Stone's role was nor where his expertise lay. Early in the conflict, in November 1914, Signals Sections from the 31st Divisional Signal Company RE were sent to Africa from India, but the majority of personnel went to Mesopotamia in April of the following year. Several Sappers remained and a Signals Section was quickly formed in Nairobi. It is possible that William Stone was one of these Sappers. Further reinforcements arrived in July 1915 from both India and Britain and a Company was formed with the title 'Z' Divisional Signal Company, Sappers and Miners, as part of the Indian Army war establishment. Though training facilities were set up in Nairobi, and Signals staff were fully involved in actions against the enemy, starved of up-to-date equipment and personnel, the size of the Company gradually declined until, in June 1917, it was disbanded with a strength of ten per cent of its establishment figure.

Again, it has not been possible to establish when William Stone left East Africa for India. Such limited documentation as exists suggests he may have been wounded and sent by sea to the main Indian Army hospital facilities in Poona. This would have necessitated a lengthy journey of two to three weeks. Other somewhat nearer hospital provision, if not in Kenya itself, could have been found in South Africa or Egypt. Alternatively he may not have been injured in East Africa but simply returned to India for further training or redeployment. No one knows. What we do know is that he died tragically of Spanish flu in October 1918.

Spanish flu reared its serious and in many cases its deadly head in March 1918. Unlike other strains of influenza that occur, that are only ever fatal in the very young, very old or very ill, Spanish flu acted differently. It seemed to target the young and healthy. In particular, it was more deadly to people aged between 20 and 35. This strain of flu soon spread around the world, affecting many millions of people and killing over 50 million throughout the world. It was reported to have spread in three waves or stages.

It is not known exactly where Spanish flu originated, but China and the USA experienced some of the first recorded cases. It is thought that infected troops from the US shipped to Europe had unwittingly brought the flu with them.

When the flu found its way to Spain, their Government announced the epidemic. As Spain was the first country that was not engaged in the First World War to be struck by the flu, its health reports were not censored.

Therefore, people only heard about this deadly strain of flu having attacked Spain first. Thus it became commonly known as Spanish Flu. The flu then spread to Russia, India, China and Africa. By late July 1918 the first wave seemed to be on the wane.

The second wave of Spanish flu, still highly contagious, was even more deadly. When hospitals became full to capacity, tent hospitals were erected. Doctors and nurses were already in short supply as so many were in Europe tending to the war casualties. Volunteers were sought. Many people, especially women, signed up despite knowing that they were risking their own lives.

The flu attacked the body with great speed. The first symptoms of headache and fever were followed by the skin turning blue. Sufferers would then cough and vomit blood, others became incontinent. Many died within a day or two of feeling unwell and in some cases within just a few hours.

As so many people died so quickly there were insufficient coffins to bury individuals. Mass graves were hurriedly dug to rid the towns and cities of rotting corpses.

With the Armistice signed, came the third wave of flu. As war-torn countries celebrated the end of four years of slaughter, joyous people turned out to hug and kiss one another and the returning servicemen. This is how the third and final wave was spread. Although it was not as severe as the second wave, it was worse than the first. It was said to have ended in spring 1919, a year or so after it had started, but some believe that it wasn't until 1920 that it eventually disappeared.

Poona was a Spanish flu 'hotspot' and sadly, on 5th October 1918, William Charles Penny Stone succumbed to Spanish flu. He was buried the next day in St Sepulchre's Cemetery in Poona, India. The service was taken by Chaplain E.E. Hill.

William's brother Ernest was more fortunate. He survived the war. He too joined the Dorset Regiment and rose to the rank of sergeant. He saw action in both Gallipoli and Ypres. He wanted to continue his career in the Army but an accident prevented that. He was invalided out of the Army. It must have been at this time that he was admitted to the Graylingswell war hospital to recover. Graylingswell war hospital was located in Chichester and was originally a mental hospital. It was requisitioned in support of the war effort to be used as a military hospital. After the war, it returned to its previous function until it closed in 2001.

In 1917, Ernest married Louisa Maud Bishop, who at the time was in service at Moreton House in Owermoigne near Dorchester. They went on to have two sons, Albert Frank, born in 1918, and Lawrence Cleeve who was born an astonishing 22 years later. Lawrence Cleeve was named after Lawrence of Arabia and brewer Cleeve Palmer because Ernest had been foreman at Palmers Brewery for many years. William and Ernest's father Edmund married his sister-in-law Ada in 1927. Their final place of residence was Stones Cottage, Nettlecombe, as it is still called today (Plate 3).

This Parish family has not died out or disappeared. Living relatives are still to be found in Nettlecombe and Bournemouth.

Edward Marsh and Edward Parham

Edward Marsh is a farmer.
Edward Parham is a retired University teacher.

CHAPTER 15

Harry Marsh
HMS Carlisle
Died Vladivostok, 22nd October 1919

THE DEATH of Harry Marsh in Vladivostok on 22nd October 1919 testifies to the diversification of the over-running war in the East, confirming the ending of the First World War to have been later than 1918. The embroidery of the tapestry of the contemporary history around him and to which he was an involuntary participant has been done deliberately. It reveals how the execution of grand strategy is dependent for its success upon a multiplicity of ordinary men drawn from all corners of the Kingdom.

Harry Marsh was born in Bradpole, West Dorset, 12th December 1894, to John (29) and Elizabeth (25) Marsh. John was a Bradpole man, Elizabeth came from Nettlecombe, an example of the tightness of the local communities, finding their partners close to home. They were married in 1890, the same year their first son, William, was born, baptised 24th October 1890 and died in January 1893. Their second son, Tom, was born 1892 and died in Yeovil 1983. Harry was the third. He was baptised in the parish Church of the Holy Trinity on 28th December 1894. Samuel, the fourth, died in Bridport in 1930, aged 33. They had an only daughter, Elizabeth, born in 1899, baptised 21st June 1899 and who died shortly after, just before her father John who died in January 1900 aged 34.

For a number of years, John Marsh worked as a general labourer until 8th June 1891 when he was employed as a horse driver by the Great Western Railway Company. For that, he was paid 16 shillings a week, increased to 17 shillings the following year. Employment was desperately difficult at this time due to the mechanisation of the agricultural industry. In 1895 he found work at Avonmouth Dock, 75 miles away, as a gatekeeper with the BP&P Line, for 16 shillings a week. In 1896, his luck changed when he found a position in his home village as gatekeeper for the Bradpole railway crossing. There was a tied cottage, Holly Cottage, later Gateway Cottage. In May 1897, his salary increased to 17 shillings a week and in May 1898 to 18 shillings a week. His widow lost not only her husband but also her home.

The 1901 census reveals her living in Middle Street, Bradpole, with her sons, Tom, Harry and Samuel. Bridport's rope and net industry relied upon the local cottage workforce. Elizabeth worked from home as a twine rope braider. In September 1902 she married farm labourer Edward Perrott, occupant of three rooms in Nettlecombe. Her new husband was twenty-two years her senior. For her, the return to Nettlecombe was a return to her roots. They had a daughter, Gladys Vera, born somewhat less than nine months after their marriage.

The 1911 census shows Edward Perrott, Elizabeth, Samuel and Gladys in Nettlecombe. Tom was traced to Pirbright where he was serving with the Grenadier Guards. Harry (16) was employed as a hewer of coal in Tylorstown, Glamorgan. At that time he was living with his uncle, Andrew Dunham, Elizabeth's brother, and also a coal hewer. Andrew's Cardiff-born wife and their six children made up the household.

Welsh coal had always been the Royal Navy's coal of choice but by 19th April 1912, when Harry Marsh joined the Royal Navy on a 12-year engagement in the stoker trade (having added an additional year to his age) times were changing. The thoughts of naval thinkers had become focused upon the possibilities offered by the steam turbine and oil fuel. Of all the maritime powers, the Royal Navy's strategic reach was least affected, due to the proliferation of coal bunkering facilities in British colonies throughout the world. Oil was the most efficient and simplest fuel to handle and therefore offered ships of all nations greater reach, notably Germany. The dichotomy of coal and other pointers towards the nature of future conflict was set out in 1904-05 when Russia and Japan fought each other in Manchuria, territory which neither owned.

Russia's principal Pacific port, Vladivostok, had the significant disadvantage of being ice-bound in winter. Manchuria's Port Arthur, Lushun, did not suffer that disadvantage. It was ice free throughout the year. The disadvantages which accrued from Russia's seizure of Port Arthur were arguably more significant. The port had a narrow, shallow entrance and was surrounded by high hills. These negative factors did not prevent Russia from basing her Pacific Fleet there.

Japan had one fleet, mostly comprising modern, British-built warships. Russia had three fleets; the Pacific Fleet at Port Arthur, the embargoed Black Sea Fleet and the Baltic Fleet. The Russians had a number of modern battleships whose effectiveness would be compromised by operating jointly with old, slow, poorly protected 'self-sinkers'.

As the war developed, the Japanese were able to advance towards the hills surrounding Port Arthur, behind which they set up batteries of 11-inch howitzers firing 500-pound shells. The Russians discovered they had occupied a shell trap from which mines and the Imperial Japanese Navy prevented their escape. It would seem unlikely that the Baltic Fleet would be called down to make rendezvous with the Pacific Fleet with the intention, between them, of destroying the Imperial Japanese Navy, but that is what happened.

En route, on the Dogger Bank, the Baltic Fleet shot up the Gamecock fishing fleet out of Hull, in the conviction they were Japanese torpedo boats. Such stupidity must not detract from the achievement of Admiral Rozhdestvenski's epic voyage. A contract with Hamburg Amerika Line provided colliers for coaling on the high seas. Unlike the British, the Russians had no strategically based coaling stations along the way. In the heat and dust in the tropics, men died among the stacks of coal, including the son of the Russian ambassador to France. As Rozhdestvenski drew nearer, the Japanese picked up the tempo at Port Arthur to ensure they would avoid facing two fleets. The captain of the last remaining Russian battleship scuttled her, leaving the Imperial Japanese Navy free to meet the ponderous Baltic Fleet one on one. The Imperial Japanese Army sank the Imperial Russian Navy's Pacific Fleet. It was not a fair fight. The Japanese comprehensively destroyed the Russians at Tsushima in what became one of the most one-sided victories in modern maritime history. The cruiser *Aurora*, which would fire the opening shot of the Revolution, fled south to Manila where she was held until the end of the war.

On land, the Russo-Japanese War was effectively the full dress rehearsal for the First World War. Observers witnessed trench warfare, the extensive use of barbed wire, the devastating effects of heavy artillery, chattering machine guns and the severe limitations of cavalry in this environment but, lessons identified became heavily layered and undeclared by observers, many with their own interest in preserving the status quo. Others had taken the view that the Russian performance had been so inept as to distort any conclusions they might have reached. The Russian public were similarly unimpressed. Protests broke out in 1905 across the country.

On 5th September 1905, the Peace Treaty was signed aboard the *Mayflower* at Portsmouth, New Hampshire, under the chairmanship of President Theodore Roosevelt. Japan received no indemnity and her territorial gains were few in what transpired to be a Russian coup. According to the *New York Times*: "The judgement of all observers here, whether pro-Japanese or pro-Russian, is that the victory is as astonishing a thing as was ever seen in diplomatic history. A nation hopelessly beaten in every battle of the war, one army captured and the other overwhelmingly routed, with a navy swept from the seas, dictated her own terms to the victor". Roosevelt had established the beginning of the fatal rivalry in the Pacific between America and Japan. For the United States, the Russo-Japanese war had a far greater impact upon the Second rather than the First World War.

Harry Marsh's enlistment documents describe him as being 18 years of age, almost 5 feet 10 inches tall, with dark brown hair, blue eyes and a fair complexion. He spent a number of months on board various training ships until assigned as a qualified stoker to *HMS Topaze* on 5th May 1914. *HMS Topaze* was rated a Gem Class, third class cruiser, serving as the light cruiser of the Fifth Battle Squadron of the Channel Fleet in 1914-1915, with the Italians in the Mediterranean 1915-1917 and in the Red Sea from March 1917 until the Armistice. Harry Marsh, a Petty Officer (Stoker) since July 1917, joined *HMS Carlisle* (Plate 33) on 7th November 1918. *HMS Carlisle* was a Carlisle Class Light Cruiser, ordered in 1916. Built at the Fairfields of Govan shipyard in Glasgow for the Royal Navy, her keel was laid down in October 1917. She was completed on 11th November 1918, Armistice Day, too late to see action in the European Theatre. She had a hangar forward of the bridge to carry aircraft. The idea never came to fruition and the hangar was removed. After her work-up, in 1919 *Carlisle* joined the Fifth Light Cruiser Squadron at Harwich. Barely halfway through his 12-year engagement, there would be no return home for Harry Marsh among the demobilised. During March, *HMS Carlisle* left Harwich with the squadron for the China Station, where she served until 1928. A fully oil-fuelled ship, she had a top speed of 29 knots.

Russian unpreparedness, poor equipment, indifferent leadership and the growing disillusionment among the rank and file were all contributing to a shockwave soon to flood and overwhelm the State. It was vital for Britain and France that Russia should remain engaged in the war against Germany. In 1917, the Russian Army was 9,000,000-strong of which 7,000,000 were directly employed at the seat of war. They had suffered 2,000,000 dead. This significant residual weight of manpower occupied the attention of 160 German divisions. Keeping Russia in the war for 3½ years imposed logistic penalties on Joffre and Haig but not as many as those faced by Germany. The Eastern Front made extreme demands upon manpower and materiel which, if it had not existed, might have been gainfully employed to tip the fine balance in favour of Germany on the Western Front. London and Paris were determined to use all necessary means to keep Russia in the war.

In March 1917 there were riots. Two million soldiers deserted during March and April. The Tsar abdicated. Germany transported Lenin and his supporters in a sealed train across Germany to Stockholm. Trotsky moved from the United States and Stalin from Siberia. Commenting in October on the scale of desertion of soldiers from the Army, Lenin said: "The Army voted for peace with its feet". The Bolshevik revolution brought Lenin to power on 7th November 1917, whereupon he sued for peace, signing the stop-start Armistice of Brest Litovsk giving the Germans vast swathes of Russian territory. The Peace of Brest Litovsk on 18th February 1918 confirmed the withdrawal of Russia from the First World War.

When all seemed lost, the White Russians, aided by an army of 70,000 former Czech prisoners of war, began to take control of large areas of the Siberian Steppes from the Bolsheviks. The War Office in London decided to send a battalion as a sign of solidarity but this had more to do with forcing the hand of a wavering President Wilson to intervene in Russia by sending US troops. The German reinforcement of the Western Front due to the collapse of the Eastern Front put the availability of British battalions at a premium. Orders were passed to the unlikely Commanding Officer of the 25th Middlesex, then in Hong Kong, to deploy his aged Dad's Army battalion of conscripts, unfit to be sent to the trenches, to Omsk in Siberia. He had, he wrote in his memoirs, "to carry out

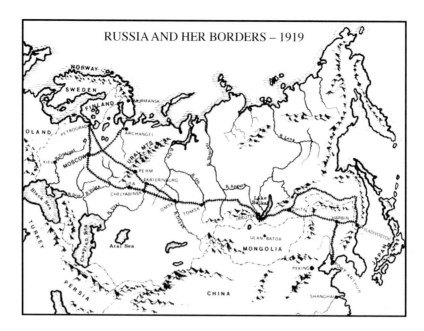

RUSSIA AND HER BORDERS – 1919

the services of a front-line service battalion with the personnel and equipment of second-grade garrison troops". That requirement was less exceptional than his involvement in the *Kolchakovshina.*

John Ward, the 52 year old commanding officer of the 25th Middlesex, began his working life at the age of nine as a ploughboy, became a railway navvy aged 12 then, still in his teens, joined the army, seeing service in the Sudan. On his return to England, aged 24, he founded the Navvies' Union. He became one of the Labour Party's earliest MPs, winning the seat of Stoke-on-Trent. This leftward-leaning man distinguished himself by protecting Alexander Vasilevich Kolchak who, for a few brief moments, seemed to be the person to succeed the Romanovs and rally Mother Russia against Lenin and Trotsky.

During the Battalion's posting to Omsk from the winter of 1918 to spring 1919, Ward took upon himself the responsibility for keeping Kolchak safe. He saw him for the first time on 6th November 1918: "The impression on my mind was that I had seen a small, vagrant, lonely, troubled soul without a friend enter unbidden to the feast". A new Government was formed that day in Omsk, after which politicians offered Kolchak the post of Supreme Ruler of Russia. As a former navy admiral, he lacked the political ability and sense to overcome his and others' mistakes. His drug habit did not help.

The examination of Kolchak's character is an essential prerequisite to understanding why he failed.

A Czech officer wrote of Omsk: "The thought kept running through my head how lonely and dreary was the stage which Kolchak had selected for his empire building. In the midst of this treeless steppe, six foot deep with snow in winter, windbound and brown in summer, when the only break in the monotony is an occasional horseshoe-shaped cluster of Tartar *yurtas*, Omsk is cut off from all civilisation. This is merely accentuated by the thin steel ribbon of the Trans-Siberian (Railway)". The British and French chose to base their Siberian presence in Omsk. British forces were also sent to northern and southern Russia. The relationship developed into an unhelpful competition for influence in Anglo-French Western Siberia.

The 14 states that intervened in Russia had their separate reasons for being there. The United States and Japan kept themselves close to the east coast, never far from Vladivostok, 'Lord of the East' and eastern terminus of the Trans-Siberian Railway. The American national commander, General William S. Graves, arrived in theatre with his mission statement in the form of an *aide mémoire* typed personally by President Woodrow Wilson. The Japanese had a hidden agenda to take any opportunity during the turmoil of revolutionary war to achieve a foothold on mainland Asia. The United States found herself divided by her aims and purpose for being in Russia. They withdrew in 1920, as did the remnants of the British force. Throughout the Cold War, the Soviets let it be known they would never forgive the interveners for meddling in their civil war.

Those who betrayed Kolchak were his supposed allies who had intervened in Russia's war for varying national reasons and whose separate aims defied coordination. When the White Russians realised that the few allied military men in their country were there to secure political and economic rather than military goals, the credibility of their intervention evaporated. Kolchak had been left stranded. There is little doubt that without the implied support of the allies, notably the British and the French, and the willing availability of the Czech General Gajda and his men, Kolchak would not have been swayed to agree to becoming Russia's Supreme Ruler. "Alas!" wrote Ward, "he waited for seven months in vain; the allies never came! After expending his last ounce of energy and getting so near to final victory, we failed him at the post. Why?"

Another British battalion, 1/9th Hampshires, was deployed in support of the Middlesex but, given the size of Siberia, it was difficult to imagine what could be achieved. They had no genuine offensive role, being an adjunct of British economic policy, just as Clive's men had been in India. The land of the Yakuts alone is the size of India. Lake Baikal, the size of Switzerland, contains a fifth of the world's drinking water. In winter, railway engineers laid tracks upon the lake's frozen surface, taking the direct route so as to avoid the circuitous southern route.

White forces continued to be successful, advancing upon Moscow where they found they lacked the impetus and resources to take the city. Overstretched and overcommitted, they were forced back along their lines of communication. In Churchill's opinion, "the Armistice proved to be the death warrant of the Russian national cause". If nothing else, it provided the British conscripts with their ticket home. The only force that could have made a difference was the Czech Legion, the former prisoners of war, left stranded by Brest Litovsk. Whilst in Siberia, they found their political soul mates among the Social Revolutionaries who had been terrorised by forces loyal to Kolchak. The Czechs owed Kolchak nothing. They began their anabasis westward to build their own new state. At Irkutsk, the French General Maurice Janin handed Kolchak to his enemies, the Social Revolutionaries, who gave him up to the Bolsheviks.

HMS Carlisle sailed from Wei-Hei-Wei on 27th June 1919 for Vladivostok on Harry Marsh's final voyage, arriving there on 1st July. The sailors found the city on a war footing. Uniforms identified those who were on their side but little could be done to identify the politics of the inhabitants, whether they were Red or White. What passed as strange was their discovery that up there, from their features, genuine Russians could look every bit like Chinese. The navy's function was one part guard ship, one part 'fire brigade', both of which involved training, and the other part social, when the Wardroom could be transformed into a floating gin palace for the entertainment of official dignitaries and senior allied officers. Otherwise, if the lower decks were to be believed, they found themselves almost continuously employed cleaning the ship.

They did go ashore and over the weeks became familiar with a lawless city beyond the confines of the docks and jetties. There were substantial buildings there, meant to last. In the hustle and bustle, single deck trams rang out their warnings on clanging bells if their drivers thought their undoubted right of way was unwisely being challenged. There was also much of the busy movement of steam locomotives for connection either to passenger carriages or goods wagons.

With autumn came the onset of cold weather, making a dull, grey city duller and a reminder that all ships should be gone before the onset of winter proper. What Harry Marsh was doing on 22nd October 1919, out by himself, walking a lonely road, will never be known. What is known is that he was shot and killed by an assailant and robbed 'whilst on shore leave'. Vladivostok had developed into a profitable centre for the redistribution of liberated jewellery and small icons among the visiting military and foreign public servants. What little amount the Marsh family were able to discover about Harry Marsh's death was that he was in civilian clothes at the time. He had also purchased a valuable diamond and ruby brooch in Vladivostok which was not among the effects returned to his mother in Nettlecombe.

There had been no heroics associated with this 28 year old's death. It had been a case of wrong place, wrong time. Two days later, at 2 pm on Friday 24th October 1919, his funeral escort left the ship for the Lutheran Section of Pokrovskaya Cemetery in Kitaisakaya Street for his funeral, returning at 3.30 pm. This cemetery became the last resting place for seven sailors of the Royal Navy, one Marine and one British soldier. The graves are no longer maintained. The Churkin Naval Cemetery was used by British, French, American and Czechoslovak troops. The Canadians erected a central monument in the British plot and on this, the Vladivostok Memorial (Plate 34), are inscribed the names of the 13 British soldiers whose graves are in other parts of Siberia.

It can be seen, therefore, that the level of British casualties could be described as light. Those who had been the first to arrive had been welcomed by the Bolsheviks. While that state of harmony could not last forever, the British did not go out of their way to take the Bolsheviks on. They had learned something General Sir Frederick Roberts had observed during the second Afghan War 1878-80. "I feel sure I am right when I say the less the Afghans see of us, the less they dislike us. Should the Russians attempt to conquer Afghanistan, we should have a better chance of attaching the Afghans to our interest if we avoid all interference with them."

On 1st November 1919, *HMS Carlisle* weighed anchor and sailed for Kobe via Hong Kong.

On 6th February 1920, Kolchak's interrogators abruptly ceased their methodical questioning of their prisoner. They feared a rescue attempt by the White forces. Before first light the next day, Kolchak, together with his Prime Minister Pepeliaev, was led from his cell in Irkutsk gaol down onto the ice of the Ushakovka, a tributary of the Anghara. In the light provided by the firing squad's vehicle, both men were shot dead, their bodies disposed of through a hole cut in the ice.

At Appleshaw, Hampshire, I found the house John Ward had built for himself after his return from Siberia, now completely overgrown. Pulling back the ivy I read an inscription:

OMSK

LT COL JOHN WARD CB CMG

MP STOKE-ON-TRENT 1920

In his mémoirs he had written: "The Statesman and the soldier rarely write history; it is their misfortune to make it".

After March 1920, with Kolchak dead and all British forces withdrawn from Russia, the time had come for the Foreign Office to close the file. Lord Hardinge, Permanent Under Secretary of State to the Foreign Secretary Lord Curzon, wrote across its cover sheet: "So ends a not very creditable enterprise". When the file came to Curzon's desk, he noted what Hardinge had written, took out his pen and amended Hardinge's comment to read: "So ends a highly discreditable enterprise".

Harry Marsh wrote no history, it had been his misfortune to make it. In her cottage in the hamlet of Nettlecombe in the Parish of Powerstock, Dorset, his mother mourned the loss of her blue-eyed boy. His name duly appeared on the Parish war memorial recording his death on 22nd October 1919, over eleven months after the Armistice. The National Probate Calendar of 1920 finalised the transfer of all of Harry's worldly goods when his effects in the sum of £110 12s 2d were passed to his mother. She died at Crabbs Coppice, Beaminster and was buried in Bradpole on 15th April 1926 aged 56.

Richard Connaughton

CHAPTER 16

Christmas 1914 on the Western Front

I TOOK a call from the late Leo Cooper. He said he had read and much enjoyed *Rising Sun and Tumbling Bear – Russia's War with Japan.* It had, he insisted, terrific potential for conversion to fiction. I demurred, telling him that if I were to write a passionate bodice-ripper I could just imagine the interrogation by my wife. He insisted there was no need to go to extremes. "Write me out three chapters as fiction and let me see it." This I did. He rang me back with the advice, "stick to non-fiction!" I recalled this anecdote after re-reading Michael Morpurgo's *The Best Christmas Present in the World,* a fictitious story written of an actual event in Flanders on Christmas Day 1914. This book has the connectivity with a reading public, young and old, which textbooks and most non-fiction cannot reach.

I have no charter for the ruination of stories for would-be readers so I shall be brief in setting out my introduction. The book is set in Bridport, West Dorset, four miles to the southwest of Powerstock. The main character bought an old desk in a Bridport shop. In a secret drawer he discovered a letter penned by a British officer from Flanders' trenches in which he recounted to his wife an account of a remarkable event on Christmas Day 1914: "Something wonderful has just happened that I must tell you about at once".

A truce had broken out. The British and Germans met in No Man's Land, shared their food, sang carols and played football – "no one dies in a football match". The British officer met his opposite number, Hans Wolf, an educated man whose favourite novel was Thomas Hardy's *Far from the Madding Crowd.* Powerstock is within Hardy Country. Bridport is Hardy's Port Bredy. Out there in the cold, the two officers "talked of Bathsheba and Gabriel Oak and Sergeant Troy and Dorset".

There is a prize winning DVD, *Joyeux Noel* (Merry Christmas), which describes in a feature film, in colour, the events of Christmas 1914. It tells the story through the eyes of the French, Scottish and German soldiers who were there. The work is said to be based on original documents, undeniably entertaining, that is if the public can accept the presence of the gowned operatic soprano in the trenches.

There is a number of reasons for the spontaneous fraternisation which gave rise to so much concern among Generals on both sides. The majority of continental soldiers would not have crossed over borders into foreign land. That is equally true, almost without exception, of British soldiers unlikely to have been abroad before. For those on both sides professing to be Christians, Christmas 1914 seems likely to be the first time they had not celebrated Christmas *en famille.* Their military colleagues became their surrogate family, none of whom could have celebrated this special day without their opponents' cooperation. The dawning of this unavoidable conclusion arose concurrently among the opposing trenches. The war was not five months old. The extent of the full nastiness it was capable of achieving had yet to be revealed to its participants.

The earliest known manifestation of the informal 1914 Christmas truce in Flanders had been a football match – more a kickabout – between soldiers of the Royal Warwickshire Regiment and Germans of a Saxony unit, the 134th, on a turnip field alongside Ploegsteert Wood (near to Ypres in Belgium), close to the French border. A solid wooden cross marks the spot, a place of pilgrimage for those English football supporters who know its location and significance. The assembly of British and Germans in no man's land had been tentative. The assurances they would be home by Christmas had been false. Most guns fell silent. Among their first tasks as they shared out cigarettes, rum and Korn and exchanged badges and buttons was to bury their dead, a task they had completed by midday. They also took the opportunity to repair their trenches. One of the Royal Warwickshires had been sent a football for Christmas – not as daft as it might seem because when they were not eyeball to eyeball with their enemy, there were moments for recreation.

Leutnant Kurt Zehmisch, in the Hans Wolf role, explained what happened. "A couple of English brought a football out of their trench and a vigorous match began. This was all so marvellous and strange. The English officers thought so too. Towards evening, the officers asked whether a big football match could be held on the following day between the two positions." The 134th were due to be relieved in place on Boxing Day. Zehmisch could not speak on behalf of his relief. Nevertheless, what had happened here made a marked impression upon him. "So after all, the Christmas festival, the festival of love, caused hated enemies to be friends for a short time." (Plate 38)

Alongside the Royal Warwickshires was a battalion of the Rifle Brigade, one of whose members, Private Henry Williamson, author of *Tarka the Otter*, in 1964 gave the BBC a classic account of the meeting between the British and Germans at Ploegsteert Wood on Christmas Day 1914.

> "We crept out, trying to avoid our boots ringing on the frozen ground, and expecting any moment to fall flat, with the machine guns opening up. And nothing happened. And within two hours we were walking about laughing and talking, there was nothing from the German side. At about 11 o'clock I saw a Christmas tree going up on the German trenches. And there was a light. And then a German voice began to sing *Stille Nacht, Heilige Nacht* (Silent Night). Somebody said 'come over Tommy, come over'. Very soon we were exchanging gifts.
>
> "The following day, the exercise repeated. The whole of no man's land was grey and khaki. There they were, smoking and talking, shaking hands, exchanging addresses to write to one another."

Whilst burying the dead, Williamson observed the Germans marking their graves with crosses bearing the words 'For Fatherland and Freedom'. "I said to a German, 'how can you be fighting for freedom? You started the war and *we* are fighting for freedom'. And he said, 'we are fighting for freedom. For our country'. The German added, 'do not let us quarrel on Christmas Day'." The truce had lasted four days, being brought to an end by an order that fraternisation must end. The Germans sent the British a note saying senior officers would be visiting that night. They would be expected to fire their weapons but would aim high.

There was a much-loved song of the British army, set in Armentières to the west of Lille wherein there were many much loved ladies. At the time of the fraternisation, the 1st Battalion The

Cameronians (Scottish Rifles) were there, their medical support provided by the regimental medical officer, Fred Davidson. Fred had a camera and during his tour of duty took many photographs of his battalion at war. The men were Glaswegians and pretty dour for that. They rejected the entreaties from the nearby German trenches to join together to celebrate Christmas. "Why do you not come and join us?" asked a voice from the German trenches. "Cause we don't trust you and ye have been four months shooting at us" replied a stern voice, ending any possibility of dialogue.

Further along the line of trenches at Houplines was the 2nd Battalion Argyll and Sutherland Highlanders who, from the accounts of their regimental medical officer Frederick Chandler, as Highlanders, were altogether a more agreeable group of soldiers than their fellow Scots from lowland Glasgow. Approximately half the British Expeditionary Force units between St Eloi and La Bassée joined with the Germans in the celebration of Christmas. Frederick Chandler wrote:

"Last night was Christmas Eve. It was a bright starry moonlit night and it froze hard. Opposite our trenches was perfect quiet and soon we began to hear the shouts of our men to the Germans and their replies. Then various musical instruments began, and song and ribald mirth. One of our sergeants got out of the trench and met one of the Germans halfway. He lived in Scotland and spoke English with a Scotch accent! They shook hands and exchanged hats, the German declaring they had no wish to be fighting the English.

Between the Welch Fusiliers and the Germans opposite them were passed greetings and words of bonhomie, and also intermittent fire, whereat I was sorry.

This morning it was still freezing hard but a heavy mist was over everything… In the afternoon all firing ceased about our lines and an extraordinary thing occurred. Our men and the Germans got out of the trenches and met each other and chatted in great groups. The Germans in fact brought a barrel of beer over to the Regt on our left! One could walk about anywhere with safety – it was a most delicious feeling I can tell you. There was still some sniping going on on our right, but later on this stopped and about 6 pm there was absolute quiet. It was perfectly delicious. I have not heard a quiet five minutes for nearly two months. Now, about 9 pm, the singing has begun again and there is still no firing. You can't imagine how sick one gets of the crack-crack of rifles and the beastly singing noise of the bullets. I swear they are worse than shells.

For dinner tonight we had soup, white wine, haggis, whisky and vegetables, some sort of old fowl, Christmas pudding with rum, a savoury, dry biscuits and café au rhum. This morning we came across a dead German. We had him buried properly and I got a couple of buttons off the poor devil. A weird Christmas, n'est-ce pas?"

On Thursday 24th December, Christmas Eve, Lieutenant William Tyrell RAMC, with a Field Ambulance in Flanders, wrote in his diary: "No peace here – guns blowing off around Ploegsteert, Messines and Rabecque". Diaries written at the time by British, Germans, French and Belgians reveal an overall sense of humanity and a keen desire to stop the war, if only for a short period in order to celebrate Christmas.

"We good, no shoot!"

"Comrades, don't shoot!"

"Just opposite, the Germans were singing a Christmas carol, interrupted and punctuated by rifle fire. Poor little God of love, born tonight, how can you love mankind?"

War Diary, Maurice Laurentin, Lieutenant,
77ème Régiment d'Infanterie, Christmas 1914

"They came out of their trenches and walked across unarmed, with boxes of cigars and seasonable remarks. What were our men to do? Shoot? You could not shoot unarmed men."

The Doings of the 15th INFANTRY Brigade, Count Gleichen,
Brigadier General 15th Brigade, 1915

Herentage Wood

"Front line, 1.1.15. 'Don't shoot!' we said to each other. We showed our faces. We laughed. We beckoned, 'Come here!' They threw packets of cigarettes. We threw back oranges and apples. A few men came out to pick up the fruit that had fallen in front of the trenches. We waved a bottle. This fair-haired Boche, strapping and smooth-faced, threw himself at everything we gave him. Soon, there were more than twenty heads showing above the trench. We didn't try to hide, either. Two Germans came up. One explained to us that it was us who should go over to them. The other suddenly exclaimed, 'Ah! I've had enough!' and jumped into our trench, where he finished his speech. 'I'm from Alsace, and I'm coming with you!' He was from the 126th."

War Diary, Maurice Laurentin, Lieutenant,
77ème Régiment d'Infanterie

"Even in the trenches, the French celebrated the new year. We heard songs and music, people beckoned to us, waving bottles of wine and throwing oranges and tobacco. Meanwhile, our pioneers took the opportunity to string barbed wire from one tree to another in front of our position."

Diary, Oberleutnant der Reserve Crönert, 1/126 I.R.

"The night of storm was followed by a sunny winter's day, which encouraged the French to leave their cold, damp trenches. We saw a group of French officers strolling and chatting and smoking cigarettes in a firebreak a few hundred metres behind their position. One of our machine guns, hastily dispatched, soon put right what we thought was this inappropriate behaviour. The peace quickly came to an end, and the indignant letters from the French about our 'unfairness' were also their last. The first had said, 'Tomorrow be on your guard; a general is coming to visit our post. We shall have to fire for honour and from shame.'"

Diary, Oberleutnant L. Bolz, 11/126 I.R.

Hill 60

"One of the lads from our company waved a placard over the trench with the inscription 'Happy Christmas'. Soon the British did the same. One Englishman called out to ask us in good German whether we wanted to take away the dead which lay between the two positions. (At that point there were between 50 and 60 dead in front of our company's sector.) After a short pause for thought, we agreed, and some of our lads left the trenches at the same time as the British. Later, the British again asked us to sing Christmas carols."

Diary, Leutnant der Reserve Meinicke, I.R. 143
St-Elooi-Wijtschate-Mesen

"The night of Christmas Eve, 24.12.14, it was my privilege to play Father Christmas and to carry a Christmas tree to my company commander in the trenches at the very front. There was a new moon, and the bright starlit sky was lit even more brightly by the tracer bullets from the two front lines. For me, they were beautiful Christmas illuminations. Nothing was heard, except machine gun fire from time to time, or a short burst of shots. Sometimes an infantryman would shoot to the left or the right of me, but I knew that the enemy would not use me as a target, despite the light which was as strong as day, because I was Father Christmas, and I was carrying the decorated tree."

Memoirs, Carl Mühlegg, 3 Komp, bayr, R.I.R. 17
Mesen-Wulvergem Road

"By breakfast time nearly all our men were on the ground between the trenches, and were the greatest pals."

Junior officer, 6ᵗʰ Cheshires

"The ball appeared from somewhere, I don't know where but it came from their side. It was just a general kickabout. I should think there were a couple of hundred taking part. I had a go at the ball. Everybody seemed to be enjoying themselves. There was no sort of ill-will between us…"

Interview, Ernie Williams, Private, 6ᵗʰ Cheshires
South of Mesen-Wilvergem Road

"December 25th. Hard fog and frost. Very quiet all day except for a little distant artillery fire. Hear that opposing trenches in one (14ᵗʰ) Brigade become friendly over cigars etc. Distributed Princess Mary's Gift Boxes. The morning was foggy, but cleared later. About 2 pm a German officer unarmed walked towards Norfolk trenches followed by others. Our men shouted to them to stop without success and so to prevent them seeing our trenches went out to meet them and for about 1½ hours 200 to 400 British and German troops including officers conversed and sang hymns together. Germans said they were not going to open fire for 3 days. Little mention of war was made. They expected it to finish within 2 months at latest."

War Diary, 15ᵗʰ Infantry Brigade, Christmas 1914

"On the days before Christmas, the British had already made approaches to R.I.R. 17 to suggest a truce. This arose quite naturally from the fact that the burial of the British dead had not been disturbed on Christmas Day. The troops came out of the trenches unarmed and gave each other presents, until the intervention of the higher command put an end to that Christmas truce. Our companies were forbidden to fraternize, but were also told not to fire unnecessarily. And now, the British were again trying their luck with us.

What happened at that time between the two fronts was an example of pure humanity."

History of the List Regiment, bayr. R.I.R. 16,26.12.14.

"One Englishman was playing on the harmonica of a German lad, some were dancing, while others were proud as peacocks to wear German helmets on their heads. The British burst into song with a carol, to which we replied with 'Stille Nacht, heilige Nacht'. It was a very moving moment – hated and embittered enemies were singing carols around the Christmas tree. All my life I will never forget that sight. We saw that men carried on living, even when they are reduced to killing and butchery… Christmas 1914 will remain unforgettable for me."

Letter to his parents, Josef Wenzl, R.I.R. 16, 28.12.14.

"Wishing you a very happy Christmas and to a speedy ending to the War!"

L.A. Praer, 1ˢᵗ Devonshire (15ᵗʰ Bde. 5ᵗʰ Div.), Christmas greetings written and handed over personally in No Man's Land to Gefreite Max Herold, 8 Kompanie R.I.R. 16.

St-Yvon

"I spotted a German officer, some sort of lieutenant I should think and, being a bit of a collector, I intimated to him that I had taken a fancy to some of his buttons.

We both then said things to each other which neither understood, and agreed to do a swap. I brought out my wire-clippers and, with a few deft snips, removed a couple of his buttons and put them in my pocket. I then gave him two of mine in exchange."

Bruce Bairnsfather, 2ⁿᵈ Lt. 1ˢᵗ Royal Warwickshires

Ploegsteert Wood

"Troops from both sides rose from their holes in the ground to stretch their legs and then to fraternise in No Man's Land between the trenches – a happy state of affairs which in our section continued for about ten days.

Many souvenirs were exchanged, ranging from buttons and badges to cigars received from the Kaiser. The prize souvenir was the celebrated 'Pickelhaube'. Our currency in this bartering was Bully Beef and Tickler's Plum and Apple, so called jam. They asked for marmalade but we had not seen any ourselves since we left England.

The following day a voice called out: "Yesterday I give you my hat for the Bullybiff. I have grand inspection tomorrow. You lend me and I bring it back after." The loan was made and the pact was kept, sealed with some extra bully."

Letter, Frank and Maurice Wray, Privates,
5ᵗʰ London Rifle Brigade

Between Le Gheer and Le Touquet

"Comical sights were to be seen. The hares on the open ground had lost their heads for certain. All of a sudden, their Eldorado was peopled with human beings. Tommy and Fritz were hunting them with one accord...Then a Scotsman brought out a football. That led to a proper match, with caps as goal posts. It had to be seen to be believed on that frozen field...The match ended 3-2 to Fritz.

On the occasion of that match, our lancers were quick to notice that the Scots were not wearing underpants under their kilts."

Letter, Johannes Niemann, Oberstlt. Sächsiche I.R. 133

Right bank of the River Lys

"The German Company-Commander asked ours if he would accept a couple of barrels of beer. They had plenty of it in the brewery. He accepted the offer with thanks and a couple of their men rolled the barrels over and we took them into our trench. The German officer sent one of his men back to the trench, who appeared shortly after carrying a tray with bottles and glasses on it. Officers of both sides clinked glasses and drank one another's health. Our Company-Commander had presented them with a plum pudding just before. The officers came to an understanding that the unofficial truce would end at midnight. At dusk we went back to our respective trenches.

'Old Soldiers Never Die', Frank Richards,
Private, 2nd Royal Welch Fusiliers

Pervijze

On Christmas Eve, the Germans placed a board beside their trenches, asking the Belgians to forget the horrors of war for an hour, in order to commemorate the birth of Christ. The Belgian soldiers were in agreement. In this way, Christmas Eve passed in an atmosphere of brotherliness. The German soldiers offered the Belgian soldiers quantities of good things, and even wine. The Belgians were embarrassed not to be able to offer anything in return. An hour later, everyone was back in the trenches. Once again, No Man's Land began to ring out with the sound of machine guns. Following this incident, a Belgian post commander, Sub-Lieutenant Naviau was shortly afterwards reduced to the ranks.

Diksmuide

"On Christmas Day, German and Belgian soldiers sang Christmas carols on the Hoge Brug at Diksmuide, and exchanged presents. The day after Christmas Day, the Belgians heard from the other bank cries of 'Kameraden, gar nicht schiessen'. The scenario of the previous day was replayed. Suddenly, three German officers under the command of Major Anderson (1872 – Somme 1916) appeared, bearing a monstrance (an open or transparent vessel in which the Host is carried in procession or exposed for adoration in Roman Catholic ceremonies) found at the hospital of St John, Diksmuide. Using a length of rope, the Belgian army chaplain Vandermeiren gently pulled the monstrance, wrapped in a linen bag, across the thin layer of ice with which the Ijzer River was covered. After which everyone returned to their places behind the front. [The allegorical painting 'Kerstnacht aan de Ijzer' (1930) ('Christmas Night on the Ijzer River') by the painter and veteran Samuel De Vriendt recalls these events. The painting hangs in the Municipal Museum in Diksmuide.]"

Bruce Bairnsfather (Personal Story – Christmas Truce)

Humour contributed strongly in sustaining the troops' morale. The British command, more than any other, grasped the importance of this. Bruce Bairnsfather, who arrived in Ploegsteert in November 1914, first of all as second lieutenant, then as captain of the Royal

Christmas Day : How it dawned for many

Warwickshire Regiment, was the greatest soldier-cartoonist of the period. It was at Ploegsteert in 1914 that he celebrated one of the many Christmas truces. He found the Christmas truce of 1914 distinctly curious, giving as his reason: "here were these sausage-eating wretches, who had elected to start this infernal European fracas, and in so doing had brought us all into the same muddy pickle as themselves... There was not an atom of hate on either side that day; and yet, on our side, not for a moment was the will to war and the will to beat them relaxed". His best-known character was Old Bill, a simple soldier with a magnificent walrus moustache. Old Bill enjoyed runaway success, not only with the British, but also with the French, American and Italian armed forces. In April 1915, suffering the effects of chlorine gas and a shell fragment wound, two 'Blighty ones', Bairnsfather was casevaced home. He continued drawing during his recuperation, sending his work to the

Bystander magazine. The War Department recognised his enormous propaganda value and as a consequence, he never returned to battle.

After the war, Old Bill was even a character on the stage and screen. Bairnsfather survived the war and died in 1959.

South of Kemmel-Wijtschate Road

"All sorts of stories have been circulated regarding the meeting of the enemy and British troops between the trenches. Luckily the troops holding our immediate line of trenches just waited until the Germans got out of the trenches, then they let them have it, rapid fire; it stopped any of this 'scratch my back and I'll scratch yours' sort of nonsense."

Diary, Bryden McKinnell, Captain
10th King's (Liverpool Scottish), 14/1/1915

It is too easy to be judgmental without being aware what these men had been through to get where they were then. Eighty-one British soldiers died on Christmas Day 1914. Among that number was Sergeant Frank Collins, 2nd Monmouthshires, shot by a sniper as he left the protection of his trench to celebrate the truce.

The truce had been spontaneous, something of the moment. Threats from Higher Commands to court martial anyone attempting to fraternise in the future had the desired effect, almost, of putting the lid on what had been, for the most part, an aberration. Some fraternising did continue in pockets through to December 1916 but it was rare and localised. Attitudes changed over a short period of time. As living conditions deteriorated beyond what would have been acceptable for animals, the human animals honed their instincts to kill those they saw as being responsible for their discomfort and as retribution against those who had killed their mates. It was almost beyond the realms of possibility to socialise with those responsible for dehumanising gas attacks on their positions. The antipathy worked both ways.

The Third Battle of Ypres, 3rd July – 10th November 1917, known as Passchendaele, saw the rain-sodden ground turned into a quagmire by three days of bombardment. Soldiers drowned in mud, their bodies lost forever. They had become used to their friends being atomised by direct or close strikes of artillery rounds but it was here, at this battle, that Germany introduced mustard gas. There had been

300,000 British, 260,000 German and 8,528 French casualties.

Those who had fraternised over Christmas 1914 had seen nowhere near the fullest extent of what unrelenting war was capable of achieving. If the British and Empire representatives present at the celebration of Christmas in 1914 had the capability of fast-forwarding the post-war images of Ypres and its surrounding area, they would have been struck by Menin Gate. In and around the Gate are carved the names of 54,896 British and Empire soldiers who died in the Ypres salient but whose bodies have never been identified or found. They would recoil at finding their names among the lost fallen. Go there. Be there at the going down of the sun, when representatives of the Ypres fire brigade sound the last post. Weep. Reflect upon the loss, the pointlessness.

Richard Connaughton

Sources:
Imperial War Museum Archives
BBC. The Great War Interviews
Flanders Fields Museum, Ieper

CHAPTER 17

We Will Remember Them

Robert Laurence Binyon 1869-1943
W. Strang. 1901

MOVED BY the early news of heavy casualties, the poet Laurence Binyon leant upon the inspirational Cornish environment to set his deepest thoughts into words. 'For the Fallen' was published in *The Times* on 21st September 1914. One verse in particular caught the public's imagination to the extent that at war's end, following the institutionalisation of Remembrance Sunday, it became and remains an essential part of the Remembrance Service. Grieving parishioners became accustomed to having the names of their fallen read out in church, accompanied by Binyon's words:

'They shall grow not old as we that are left grow old:
Age shall not weary them, nor the years condemn.
At the going down of the sun and in the morning
We will remember them.'

At the end of which the congregation responded in unison:

'We will remember them'.

The difference between now and then is that in 1920 the respondents were in a position to *remember* those lost because they had known them. It is not possible to remember that which

166

is unknown. The names heard by Powerstock's 2013 congregation were those of total strangers. A pledge was accordingly made to the effect that in a year's time, at the Centenary Remembrance Sunday, the Parish's long forgotten servicemen would be both known and remembered. We would write a book, *A Dorset Parish Remembers 1914-1919*. In November 2013 the structure began to be assembled to achieve that aim.

There would be two Groups, researchers and supporters. Seventeen researchers and writers were responsible for background material and the preparation of profiles for each of the eleven adopted war dead. The writers had until the end of April 2014 to complete up to 10 pages on their chosen person. Mary Connaughton was the first line of support. She trawled genealogy sites with a view to producing a dossier of facts on each of the individuals, facts to be set in their context. Gina Connaughton began her work as soon as manuscripts arrived. She set out each contribution in a regular format, standardising, for example, times, dates and use of italics.

Preceding all that was the design and selection of the cover. Chris Day began a process completed by Steve Luck. He is a photographer and designer whose tasks included mapping and improving the resolution of century-old photographs. Channy Kennard, the Powerstock correspondent of the Benefice Magazine, became the publicist. Among her tasks was keeping the project in the public eye with particular emphasis placed on recruiting sponsors. The £1300 raised here was set aside to go towards the settlement of the printer's early bills. Most of this income was gift-aided. Gina e-mailed the manuscripts she had checked to Margaret Morgan-Grenville, editor of the Benefice Magazine and owner of her own small publishing company. Margaret converted the incoming manuscripts to pdf format as required by the printer selected as partner in our self-publishing project.

I set out the project's rules in our obligatory Charter – obligatory, that is, if grants are to be sought. The names of the appointed officers appear in this document. On the committee were Tim Connor, our accountant and researcher, who is also the Parochial Church Council's (PCC) treasurer. Our accounts became a sub-account of the PCC's account. As will be revealed, this sensible, administratively convenient measure proved problematic. Trevor Ware was the business manager. A businessman by profession, he also had access into Bridport's Arts community. Among Trevor's principal responsibilities were pricing and aspects of marketability.

The adoption of a centralised democracy regime was intended to allow writers and supporters the maximum opportunity to focus upon their tasks. We held one 'mingle' in our pub of choice, more a group social, and one formal meeting intended to orientate the group with the concept of activities. For the most part, communication was by telephone or one-on-one in the pub to discuss specific issues. When it became known that help and guidance were required, the services of the more experienced were deployed where needed.

May and June were reserved for proof reading and the production of the final draft. The delivery of books, due at the end of July, was intended to coincide with the Parish Fête, an opportunity for early sales to buyers whose purchases would help offset costs. The formal book launch was arranged for 22nd October 2014 in the Bridport Arts Centre, a springboard to Remembrance activities 2nd-24th November 2014.

A not-for-profit venture such as this has to be aware of all available means of raising funds. Nothing is guaranteed. There is a whole raft of organisations out there offering grants. It seemed at times the hurdles we had to negotiate were impossibly high. I had to write an (admittedly assisted) five-page Equal Opportunities Charter to satisfy one organisation. The Heritage Lottery Fund makes grants of £3000-£10,000 available for First World War projects. We made an unwelcome discovery that grant applications must have their own separate bank account registered in the name of their Organisation. We had a workable arrangement with our PCC. The only way open to us to have any prospect of accessing Lottery Funds was to identify our project as the Powerstock Parochial Church Council! We had already observed among a number of grant-givers a reluctance to make grants available to churches. This is one potential bear-trap to avoid. All is not lost. The jury is still out.

One comes to the end of a journey such as this with a wealth of lessons learned. I am particularly taken by the fragility of history – how, but for the contribution of one person, part of our history might never have been told, or could have been misrepresented. Time waits for no one. If opportunities are not seized, historical records disappear into oblivion. Had we waited another year before recording experiences, this book would be marginally different.

A great deal of what we know has been passed down through the relatives of the individuals being researched. There is fragility too in that linkage, so susceptible to being broken.

Veronica Stone was known to all as Ve. Her place in this puzzle of ours is as the widow of William Stone's nephew. Farmer Edward Marsh discovered her living in Bournemouth. She was unwell at the time and he dared not press her for the information and photographs she said she had in her attic.

Edward's patience was rewarded. They became friends. In mid-May 2014, Ve came to Nettlecombe where the Stones Cottage is. Her family took lunch in the Marquis of Lorne. She felt some spookiness in the place due to finding the long-deceased William Stone looking down on her. Landlady Tracey Brady had set out along the walls of the Lounge the collection of centre pages taken from the *Bridport News* and accumulated each week as a result of the Parish's researchers revealing the outline story of their adopted Serviceman. Among them was William – an experience so unexpected, so incredibly moving.

Edward Marsh tells of her infectious enthusiasm and *joie de vivre*. She ran the London Marathon in 2013. Ve said how much she felt she was among friends in a hamlet where her relatives had roots. "I shall be coming to the Fête and I certainly would not miss Remembrance Sunday this year." Sadly, she achieved neither of those wishes. On 6th June 2014, D-Day, Ve Stone's cancer finally overwhelmed her. She died just short of her 71st birthday.

What is remarkable of this Memorial experience of ours is the bond that developed between the team, among individuals formerly strangers one to another within their own community. There was also an identifiable bond between researcher and researched. Superimposed on all this was the contribution of relatives who represented all that was there to be known of our fallen, of lives which otherwise were destined for total anonymity.

To Stuart and Michael, Ve's sons, we extend our sympathy and express our gratitude for their mother's invaluable contribution to our project. Let the permanence this record has now achieved be our tribute to her and to all the other contributors. There could be no more appropriate ending to this story than Ve's funeral at Litton Cheney conducted by the Reverend Elaine Marsh, mother of Edward Marsh.

LIST OF SPONSORS

There were those within the community who, whilst not having been directly associated with the Research and Administration Teams, let it be known that they wished to be seen to be supportive of the ideals and principles embodied in *A Dorset Parish Remembers.* They did this through kind financial contributions with which to defer the overall cost of the Project. Those individuals, the most generous of the generous, are:

John Best
Penny Best
Michael and Liz Crabb
Annie Crutchley
John Fairbairn
Graham and Gillian Fowler
Brian and Sue Galpin
Channy Kennard
David Kennard
Anthony Morrissey
Powerstock Cider Festival
Leo and Brenda Sharp
Charles Tuke
John and Vanessa White

INDEX

This index refers to local people and their places whether in England or abroad. The names of Bismarck, Brest Litovsk, Churchill, Haig, Kitchener, Joffre, Versailles etc., necessary in the text, do not appear here. The names of those who died are in **bold**, and those who served are underlined.